THE ART OF
KICKING ASS

Elegantly

IN BUSINESS, IN LOVE, IN FITNESS & IN LIFE

MICHELLE HEXT

Dedication

To Dave... the love of my life...I still can't believe we found each other and how perfectly we fit. Having you in my life allows me to soar higher than I ever have before....your patience knows no bounds and for that I'm truly grateful.

I love you more! xox

To my kids Cody and Chloe...I love you to the moon and back and couldn't be prouder if I tried.

To my mum...always my biggest fan and as I walk deeper into my 40's with 2 teens I now have a full appreciation of the hell I put you through. I love you and thank-you for thinking everything I do is totally amazing x

To my friends...you keep me sane, you keep the laughs coming and remind me of why I love being a woman...there IS no better thing than a girls night out filled with bubbles and laughing until you pee your pants.

I love you x

Lastly to my entrepreneur female sisterhood –

I wrote this book for you. Everyday I see your successes along with your struggles…we are real, we are courageous, we are resilient, we are kind and we are supportive…we cheer for one another and have a shoulder ready whenever anyone needs it.

I couldn't think of a better sisterhood to be part of if I tried.

You rock!

Contents

Introduction

Think about the last time you felt hot; you know the feeling, a happy mix of sexy and elegant and glowing with confidence and good health.

Think of the last time you felt successful in business; you know the feeling, you're in flow, everything you touch turns to gold, you're the hottest thing in your industry and you're making money hand over fist.

Imagine you have intense, deep, soul-connecting love, you're rocking the perfect body, and you have a social life to die for.

You're living the life you dreamed of.

Now picture your perfect life...*a day* in your perfect life.

Imagine that in your entrepreneurial life you have discovered your BIG IDEA, created something wonderful, and it is the raging success you dreamed it would be.

Your working days are filled with projects and people you love.

There is no chasing, no rushing, no fear and no franticness; you work in a relaxed state of flow...you are in a state of ***elegant hustle***, relaxed yet powerfully productive and strategically focused.

Imagine you love your work, but your work is NOT your No. 1 Priority...(I know right!).

You gain pleasure from your work, and you're proud of your success, but you have so much more going on in your life than just your work. As they say, no one ever died wishing they had spent more time at work.

Imagine luxury-filled, romantic weekends away, soul-filled Friday night bubbles with the girls and long glamorous lunches with your besties.

Life is not just for living, ladies; life is for *enjoying.*

Want a glimpse into my life as a glamour-loving, martial arts training, business-loving entrepreneur?

Today is a good example, so let's start there.

I woke up this morning in my beautiful, light-filled bedroom, rolled over and snuggled up to the man I love. Snuggles turn into "special time," and I can't think of a better way to start the day.

I make my man his lunch and a coffee to take on his trip to work then hit the treadmill for 40 minutes of intervals.

Still in my sweaty state, I make my breakfast (I know you're going to ask so here it is...oats made with water, choc protein powder, coconut oil and coffee) and eat this while I check my emails and go over the list of things I need to get done for the day.

Shower time...I pump up some tunes, shower then carefully dress for my 11 a.m. meeting with the publisher of a magazine I now regularly contribute to.

Heels, boyfriend jeans, Zara top, big-ass diamond ring, simple silver necklace, slim black watch, understated makeup, hair curled and pretty...I'm good to go.

I head in to the meeting a little early to get started on this introduction...yep, you read it right. I'm sitting in a lovely little cafe overlooking beautiful gardens with the sun shining as I write this intro and wait for the publisher to arrive.

After my meeting, I'll head back to my office, check emails then change into my workout gear and hit the gym.

Next on the agenda is my physio appointment, and then I'll have time to shop for dinner, spend some time at my desk, catch up with the kids and even thrown on a load of washing!

In the evening I sit down to a healthy meal cooked by my man (he is THE BEST cook and loves to do it, I know...you hate me now, don't you?!)

We relax over a beautiful glass of red and head to bed...more often than not for more special time.

Some days I run events in glamorous locations, some days I'm in client meetings (in glamorous locations) and other times I'm working from my lovely home office.

Either way there is no rushing, no stress and my days are a lovely mix of training, working and glamour...just the way I like it.

Now let me take you back to my life a little over two years ago...

My (now ex) husband wakes up, and I pretend I'm asleep so I don't need to converse with him. No need to worry about him putting "the word" on me because we now both know he shouldn't bother.

I drag myself to my office, already dreading the 100-plus emails I know I will need to deal with, knowing that many of them will be answering the same three questions over and over again, leading me to tear my hair out!

I have breakfast, get some more work done then have my shower...my bathroom was an abomination...there are no words to describe just how UN-glamorous that bathroom was...eeew!!

I put my workout gear on and hit the gym.

I come home and spend another bazillion hours working my way through my emails.

I head to my Taekwondo school to teach classes then drive home.

I drink two glasses of wine (not fussed about what) at my desk (yep, still working) to numb my loneliness, try to get away with minimal interaction with my (now ex) husband, go to bed where we don't touch - not even once - and I wake a few times during the night because the life I am living is slowly killing me.

I was miserable...in my marriage, in my work, in the lack of adventure and excitement in my life.

I was stuck, and I had no idea how I was going to get myself out of the mess I had created for myself, but I knew I had to start somewhere.

I ended my marriage.

This signaled the beginning of a very trying four months that required all of my resolve to get through...I knew my new life was just around the corner, and I just had to hang on.

I spent four months sleeping on my son's old single bed in my office, avoiding any and all contact with my ex. It was a very miserable existence.

It also happened that I had hip surgery scheduled at the same time. After my surgery I headed home to Cody's old single bed and well...it wasn't a fun time. I didn't want to ask my ex for help, and he wasn't all that keen to give it.

Thankfully I have wonderful girlfriends who helped out in those first few days and took me wherever I needed to go (mostly to the gym!).

Over the following 16 months I created the life and business I had dreamed of for close to two decades, and in the following pages, I'm going to share with you how I did it and how you too can create the very best version of your life.

A life in which you're Kicking Ass Elegantly in all of the areas of your life that matter.

Okey dokey...let's get cracking!

The Art Of Kicking
ENTREPRENEURIAL Ass

When I dare to be powerful, to use my strength,
in the service of my vision, then it becomes less
and less important whether I am afraid"

Audre Lorde

The Art Of Kicking ENTREPRENEURIAL Ass Elegantly is a state of *leisurely hustle*, where frantic no longer lives and you're in flow, doing what you love, what you're good at and being paid handsomely for it.

Simplicity - Elegance - Excellence, relaxed yet powerfully focused...all with a touch of glamour and elegance.

The entrepreneurial mind often resembles a web browser (Chrome, of course) with 78 tabs open, all vying for attention, jumping from one thing to another in a flurry of fruitless activity disguised as productivity

We equate busy-ness with productivity when often the two could not be further apart.

I used to take great pride in the amount of "stuff" I could cram into each day; I mean if I'm busy I'm successful right?

We equate busy-ness with success, when the reality is you don't need one to have the other.

It is time to get off the busy-ness treadmill and simplify.

It is time to STOP trying to achieve 37 things at once and learn the art of the elegant hustle.

Between 2012 & 2013 my income doubled.

I chased hard, I made shit happen, I did whatever it took, I worked like a woman possessed...and it worked.

Between 2013 & 2014 my income tripled.

At the very start of the year I was thrown a massive curve ball relating to my daughter's health, and from then on I was dealing with some heavy-duty challenges that often had me on my knees. I made the most of any time I managed to make myself focus on my work.

There were many days I would sit at my desk and draw a blank.

2013 had been amazing, and I was so excited about where 2014 was taking me. I had set some huge goals for myself and was chaffing at the bit to get things underway, including the launch of a new online program.

For the life of me I couldn't make it happen, and the stress caused by this lack of productivity coupled with the ongoing challenge I was dealing with was mounting.

Thankfully, I had booked a training holiday in Thailand that landed smack in the middle of the year and pulled me out of the stressful environment I had found myself in.

In Thailand, my days followed the same routine.

I was up early to spend time journaling and reflecting before I wandered down the road to my favourite restaurant for a healthy breakfast where I took my time to fully enjoy my meal, since there was no rush. Sometimes I'd take two hours to just sit and enjoy my meal and journal. Then I'd meet my Thai trainer named Thai (nope, not kidding) for a Muay Thai session: tough, challenging, fun, inspiring and energising.

More food, and again no rush to hurry on to the next thing.

Some more time for journaling and reflecting then off to the gym for some intervals and weights.

More food, then I'd wander down and have a 2-hour massage before heading to bed to read.

I was asleep by 9:00 p.m. most nights.

Usually when I'm away from home I love the travel, but I'm equally happy to come home.

This time I was deeply emotional at the thought of going home. I had come to realise just how much pressure I was under at home. While I was immersed in it every day I could deal with it day by day but having stepped out of the stress and anxiety, I was struggling with the thought of stepping back into it.

I was actually fearful of having to deal with the same things I'd been dealing with all year...a whole new world for me when usually I tackle everything head on.

I could now clearly see just how bad I'd let my stress levels become.

So what is a girl to do?

Well, this is what I did...

I listed the areas of my life:

- Business

- Love

- Training (for me this means training, my nutrition and how my body looks and feels)

- Connection

- Family / Home

I then rated each of these out of 10 in relation to my stress levels, and it looked like this:

- Business **9/10**

- Love **0/10**

- Training **0/10**

- Connection **2/10**

𝄞 Family / Home **9/10**

From here I could clearly see that my stress was stemming from business and family.

In an effort to regain some semblance of control, I decided I'd focus on controlling the "controllables" and that started with my business.

What was I worrying about specifically? It came down to being behind schedule with my launch, so I reworked my timeline, created a massive action plan (complete with a checklist), and immediately felt in control of my business again.

I knew the challenge with my daughter wasn't going to resolve any time soon and that we were in for a long road ahead, so again I looked at the controllables.

I made the decision to worry when I needed to worry and only then. I made a decision to put aside any thoughts of "what if" or imagining worst case scenarios and just focus on the immediate issue at hand then move on.

Through this I was able to see that life was far less out of control than it felt and in reality there was only one thing I was dealing with that was out of my control and once I placed some rules around how I would deal with this my stress reduced.

This new perspective changed everything for me, and I doubt very much I would have had the clarity of distance to see this in any hurry had I remained in the stressful environment back home.

I became extremely protective of the mental and emotional state I was able to cultivate in Thailand, and when I came home I was determined to bring my Thai, blissed-out state with me and to integrate into my daily life.

When I returned a funny thing happened.

Nothing had changed yet **everything** changed overnight.

Within two months of being back home, I smashed through all of the targets I had set myself and then some.

And I was working less - much less.

And money started rolling in......effortlessly and more consistently than ever before!

$20,000 months became a regular thing overnight and only continued to build from there.

I had already discovered the power of focusing on one single thing and following it through till the end.

I had defined my niche, created a product funnel that spoke to my market, was across the content my market demanded and my offerings were on point but I had become so overwhelmed that I was unable to see how I could practice the process of One Single Focus in the daily running of my business.

Thailand allowed me to get back in touch with this at a time I really needed to.

Here is the actual **ART** part...how I tripled my income by applying **the Art of Simplicity**.

The **KISS** Principle (Keep It Simple Sweetie)

I've found that the biggest mess we get ourselves into is trying to do too many things at once.

This only serves to overwhelm us and creates a head full of noise.

We wonder why we can't seem to finish anything or follow through but really, is it any wonder??!

My single biggest "success" tip is this...focus on one thing, and only one thing at a time instead of becoming distracted when you don't get the result you want immediately.

This one thing turned everything around for me in relation to productivity, enjoyment and financial reward.

Many times I had tried to adopt this approach but got drawn into another exciting idea when I was bored with the old one. I knew I had to fully embrace this idea of "one single thing", but nothing changed until I disciplined myself to actually practice it.

Don't worry I still had a bazillion other bright, shiny new ideas popping up every day, and every day I was tempted to jump on that particular passing bus BUT I dutifully noted this exciting new idea and then went back to finishing what I had started.

For YEARS I'd been following my nose and jumping from one awesome idea to the next without taking full advantage of the opportunity I had just created.

I cringe now at how close I came to ridiculous success over and over again but got bored or lost interest and chased the next thing.

From my vast experience I'm here to tell **you this no workie**!!

You can (and probably should) explore these other exciting ideas you have, BUT only once you've 100% followed through on your current one.

Think about it for a second...imagine only having to focus on ONE THING and doing that one thing well.

Imagine that all of your social media efforts are focused on only one thing...one thing you are 100% clear on, 100% committed to, 100% focused on and 100% passionate about.

Imagine only focusing on a single product funnel for a single idea for an entire year...I know, COMPLETE MADNESS!! ☺

Imagine having to only focus on getting one online program, e-book or coaching package out into the world?

One single focus = simplicity AND simplicity = finished!

DECIDE

Right now...today...**DECIDE** that you are going to give your full ENTREPRENEURIAL attention to one-single-idea.

For now decide that *this* is your focus.

Now decide to give it a year...it will take this long to fully see the potential of your idea, so prepare to dig in for the long haul.

By nature we are ideas people and because we are super smart ladies, 98% of them are good.

In fact, if we wanted to, we could turn most of them into a successful business.

But will we?

Do we?

The short answer is no.

This is also known as **TNSTS** or "the next shiny thing syndrome," and it's an affliction we need to rid ourselves of like the plague because TNSTS is death to true financial success.

I struggled with this concept for such a long time; I'd been running with TNSTS way of doing things for well over a decade but it was time to try something new, since things weren't working out the way I'd hoped.

My motivation for seeing my idea through to the end wasn't just the pride of finally seeing something through from start to finish but also knowing that once I had created it and its systems, I could then be free to add the next string to my bow.

What you're holding in your hands is an idea that formed when I started writing my first book in early 2012.

This is a freaking miracle for me; I sat on this book for close to three years, unheard of!

This book is far better than the one I would have produced had I scratched that itch 3 years ago because then I had anticipated the level of success I have right now and it was well on its way but now I have it, I'm living it. I had anticipated having a glamorous, fun, adventurous life and now I have even more of it. I had anticipated great love in my life, and now I have it.

I had the knowledge back then, but now I have a better vantage point and a deeper understanding of how to simplify things even further than I did back then.

So trust me when I say that the best business decision you can make right now, the one that will propel you forwards at a great rate of knots, is to decide on a single focus for the next 12 months. You're welcome. ☺

Ok, so what is this thing you will be focusing on for the next 12 months?

Is it something you've stopped and started, or is it something entirely new?

Whatever it is, write it down as follows:

I will focus on _____ and only _____ for the next 12 months.

I refuse to be distracted by TNSTS and any fabulous, new ideas that come to me will be hosted in The Vault until this thing is done.

My idea IS brilliant, and there IS a market waiting on me to deliver it with gusto.

I acknowledge there will be fear, doubt, second-guessing, tears and quite possibly snot.

But I will not quit.

This is my thing, and I'm going to see it though till the end.

Now print that sucker out, sign your name at the bottom and put it where you will see it EVERY SINGLE DAY!

The line is now firmly drawn in the sand, and it's time to move on to the next step.

BE STRATEGIC

Strategic = unhurried = a far more relaxed and enjoyable life.

Here's the other missing link.

Too often we operate under the practice of **FIRE - AIM – READY**, and this is NOT a good idea despite popular opinion.

What do I mean by this?

You've heard the gurus talk about JUST LAUNCH and figure it out as you go.

OR

You only need to create the first module because then you can create the rest once people sign up.

BAD IDEA!

Here's why...what happens is this thing takes off without you, and you're always playing catch up since you weren't prepared in the first place and that's if anyone signs up in the first place.

Besides, it's **unprofesh**!

I've done it, and I'll never do it again. The steps I jumped over before launch were the things that would have made the product an even greater success, or in some cases ANY kind of success!

Jump ahead, and there is a good chance you're sacrificing success (or greater success) and then you're back at square one once again.

I was at an event listening to Denise Duffield-Thomas, author of Get Rich Lucky Bitch (must read!), and what she said rocked my world.

Nothing earth-shattering and I'm sure I'd heard them before, but the timing was obviously perfect because I well and truly heard it this time.

She said (I'm paraphrasing), "*No idea is bad. Every single woman in this room has the ability to achieve great success. Why people don't succeed is because they give up.*"

Think about it...how many times have you pulled the pin on something that seemed like an incredible idea in the beginning until you let self-doubt overwhelm and derail you?

It happens to the best of us.

It happened to me too (often), but this time round I made myself stick firm and followed through till the very end.

Was I convinced my product was 100% right?

Was I convinced I had nailed my target market and knew their wants and needs?

Was I convinced there even was a market?

Hell no to all of that.

But I stayed focused and on the path anyway, and I'm so glad I did.

KNOW YOUR MARKET

Too many people skip this part.

They think they know their market, but often they only know them in a superficial way.

Yup...women...in their 30's...who want to look good.

Awesome start but nowhere near deep enough.

You need to get intimate with your market and dig deep until you fully understand their darkest fears and deepest desires.

There are many programs that teach you to drill down on this stuff (Marie Forleo does this well in her B-School), but it can be a tedious process.

If you look closely you'll often see that your target market is either A: yourself or B: someone you know.

Grab a pen and paper and write a story about them, searching for a complete and remarkable solution to a problem they have.

What are their struggles?

What do they want most in life?

What do they dream of?

What is success for them?

I find this far a more enjoyable and far more insightful process to uncovering my target markets needs and wants than trying to second guess the TV shows she likes or the magazines she enjoys reading, etc.

You know this person somewhere, somehow; that is why you came up with THIS particular idea and this particular market in the first place.

Is it going to be 100% correct?

Is every challenge or desire going to be the same across the board in your market?

Nope, it isn't. But you aren't going to let that stop you moving forward, are you??

Will there be things you missed or got wrong?

Yep, no doubt about it.

Will this make the difference between success and failure?

No...it won't.

Start with as much information and gut instinct as you can muster and then sharpen and refine as you go - the adjustments will be small and worth making as you hone in.

FINAL WORD: You can't speak to your market if you don't know what keeps them up and night and what inspires them and you can't speak to your market if you don't speak their language. This is where to spend your time if your product or service isn't hitting the mark.

YOUR PRICING

There's a whole book in this too!

The price we charge from here on in is decided on based on the value we think we provide.

In fact, the price we charge SHOULD be based on the value we KNOW we provide.

Think about that for a moment.

Have you been pricing based on your competitors or industry norms, or are you charging by the hour?

If so, then those days are over for you, my friend, because from now on we set prices based on **value** and **outcome**.

At my taekwondo school, I know what value I deliver and what outcome is derived through training in Marital Arts at MY centre (NOT the industry norm).

When I doubled my prices the only difference in conversion was an INCREASE.

The difference in attendance and retention was off the charts because my students valued their training far more than they would had I charged $5 a session.

Like it or not, most people equate expensive or premium with VALUE...HIGH value and cheap or inexpensive with low value.

It's simple, we pay more, we value it more.

When a gym throws in a handful of PT sessions with a new membership, half the time the clients don't even show up; they don't place any value on this service because neither does the gym, otherwise they would charge for it.

At the end of my PT career, I was charging $170 a session and everyone turned up when they were supposed to because of the value they placed on the service.

Were my clients paying $170 for 45 minutes of my time?

Nope.

My clients were paying for the outcome that training with me would deliver them.

When I met with a potential client, I immediately put them in vision and clearly spelled out how we were going to get them there.

I made it clear there were things I wouldn't tolerate and that I only worked with people who were as committed as I was to the outcome.

I knew my value and I made damned sure my clients knew my value too.

I knew the value placed upon living in a body they could be proud of, the change in outlook on life this would bring about, the increased energy, the improved relationships, the fact they no longer had life on hold "until."

If you are in bad shape and hate everything about the way you look and feel, how much do you think you would pay for that outcome??

Whatever it is...that is what you should charge for your service.

The same goes for my business programs.

Hell, if 10 years ago I had the kind of knowledge I'm dishing out now (based on expensive mistake after mistake), I would have saved myself years of running around in circles and hundreds of thousands of dollars.

I know the value I deliver, and I have no issue charging accordingly.

The best thing you can do right now is get clear, real clear - as in 100% clear - on what value you deliver.

Then...get confident, real confident - as in 100% confident - that you can deliver it and deliver it well.

This way you remove any negative energy around your offering, and this allows you to offer it without hesitation so it no longer feels like "selling"...and we like that!

Whatever your offering is, spend some time thinking about the outcome you deliver and what value this holds for your potential client. Come up with a $$ figure and sit with it for a few minutes.

Use your gut to guide you and then go test the market.

FINAL NOTE: When you set a scary high price, you may freak out and tell yourself, people can't afford THAT!!

People CAN afford it and so long as your market can see the value, they will pay it.

Have the kajonies to put it out there knowing the value is there and see what happens. ☺

YOUR OFFERING

For anyone to spend the big bucks on your product, they need to KNOW, LIKE and TRUST the hell out of you.

We know this right?

Did you know that it takes roughly 7 hours and 11 touch-points for someone to convert?

True story.

So what does this mean?

It means that we need to create a product funnel to guide them through those 7 hours / 11 touch-points quickly.

How do we do this?

Here are some examples of the opportunities you can provide to help them move through those 7 hours and 11 touch-points.

- Books

- E-books

- Video trainings

- Blogs

- Email newsletters

- Webinars

- Phone call

- Facebook and other social media

Spend some time thinking about how your market likes to receive information and then go ahead, start creating it and get it out there!

Here is the product formula that has worked for me to move people through.

1. **Freebie** - This is given freely and without strings, meaning you aren't attempting to capture contact details; you just want your market to see it and experience your genius and grab a quick win.

   Gifts can be the chapter of a book (they can opt to get another chapter), your blog, your YouTube channel, free, downloadable worksheets on your website...these are just a few ideas to get you started. ☺

2. **Low Risk / Low Cost Taster** - Here an opt-in is required, and these offerings can be either free or low cost.

   ⋏ A free or low cost video training series.

   ⋏ An information product.

   ⋏ A free discovery session.

   ⋏ Your book.

   ⋏ Webinars.

   The aim is to move potential clients from interested to active. The risk is low, and this is an opportunity to move them through your funnel with valuable content.

3. **Next Step Offering** - This will sometimes be bypassed if you've done a great job in the previous steps, but here you charge more and give more.

   This could be your core offering (up next) if you don't have a high-end premium product.

   Otherwise, this is your next level program or service.

   My Let's Do Lunch events and online programs are next step offerings.

4. **Core Offering / Investment Piece / Your Signature Program (your Eiffel Tower)**- This is where we hit the big bucks, so this is where your offering MUST be a COMPLETE and REMARKABLE SOLUTION to your

clients greatest challenges with more WOW than you can poke a stick at.

This will be the thing you do best and what you are (or will be) most known for.

For me this is my 12 Month Luxury Business & Lifestyle Mastermind Program http://theartofkickingasselegantly.com/mastermind/.

5. **What Next Offering** - Not everyone will require this, but if you run a program that will end at some point, your clients may not be ready to stop working with you. This is where you develop a product to allow continued support. It could be a Quarterly Alumni Mastermind or an ongoing monthly membership of some type.

The party does not need to be over so long as each of you wants it to continue the dance. ☺

Do you have something that resembles this?

Yes?

You go girlfriend!!! Refine if you need to but if it's working don't change a thing!

No?

Then you have some work to do sister!!

Spend some time mapping out your funnel in a strategic way.

Look at the examples I've given above, and fill in the gaps in your own funnel.

Once you're done, create a "to-do" list of all of the content you need to create and get cracking!

This chapter could go on for years...creating the perfect opt-in, working your list, building your tribe through social media, etc.

I'm not going to tackle every single element that makes for a successful business in this book, but instead give you key concepts and formulas that work WHEN YOU DO THEM.

Overwhelm is a killer and "aint nobody got time fo dat," so keep a clear head, work through the stuff in this chapter and let me leave you with my top five tips for entrepreneurs.

My Kickass Tips For Female Entrepreneurs.

Being an entrepreneur is a tough gig sometimes and NOT for the faint hearted. You will (if you don't already) question your sanity on an almost daily basis and frequently wonder why you thought this was a good idea in the first place.

Any long-term entrepreneur who's been in the game a while has pretty much seen it all: they've witnessed many a women who seemingly "had it all;" the great idea, the fabulous branding, kickass contacts and a rockstar personality, fail, for no apparent reason.

They've also scratched their head in wonder at how THAT woman managed to generate THAT kind of income with THAT idea.

While it is one crazy ride of highs and lows, every single one of us wouldn't hesitate to say jump in and give it your best shot, sista.

We've seen it all, we've often experienced it all, and those of us who are seasoned watch for "the cycle."

We know when someone is about to drop off, we know when someone is struggling to gain clarity, we know when a woman is stuck and can't make herself get moving again, we know when the self-doubt creeps in....and we know that when a woman is seemingly oozing success from every pore what we see is usually not a true reflection of what's really going on. Not because a woman is being deceitful, it's just that she lives in an almost constant state of optimism, a required trait for female entrepreneurs.

The benefit of having been in this game for more than two decades is this...perspective.

Here is the secret sauce I wish I had when I first started out; this is wisdom I continue to fall back on in the dip that lies between the highs.

IF YOU CONCEIVED IT, THERE IS A MARKET, YOUR IDEA IS GOOD.

Your communication of said idea may not be.

Your branding may not be.

Your delivery method may not be.

Your promotional strategy may not be.

Your distribution strategies may not be.

Your product offering may not be.

Your market may not be.

Your pricing may not be.

But your idea is, it's GOOD...so keep tweaking, test the market, find out what they want, hone your skills, get some help but **do not quit**!!

Too many ideas have fallen by the wayside because women quit before they have truly exhausted WHY their idea isn't flying.

It's usually not the idea but any combination of the above.

YOU ARE YOUR BRAND SO POSITION YOURSELF ACCORDINGLY.

Here's the deal...

We know ourselves intimately, we know how we think, and we know what our intentions are...your market does not.

Why is this important?

I'll use my mastermind program as an example.

My 12 Month Luxury Business & Lifestyle Mastermind is priced at the premium end of the market and is aimed at women just like you: ambitious, entrepreneurial, most likely well-versed in the mastermind concept and know they aren't cheap, but you also know the value is immense (if you find the right one). How would you feel about my product if I turned up at one of my Let's Do Lunch events with the ass hanging out of my pants (hypothetically of course, I'd be on to that!) and quite clearly "not there yet."

Not being a true representation of your brand is damaging, and it's difficult to come back once the damage is done.

If I were a high-end personal trainer whose job was to whip you into shape and make you look fabulous but I had an extra 10kg hanging over my Lululemon's, how damaging do you think that would be?

Imagine a brand strategist with a crappy logo, a hairdresser with fried hair, a cosmetic surgeon with a face like the Bride of Wildenstein...ummm...no thanks!

You may "intend" to get in shape, wear nicer clothes or design a better logo, but your market only sees what is in front of them right now and this is what they are basing their impressions on.

Also, be very careful who you align with because this affects your positioning in a big way. Don't grab onto any partnership that comes along simply because it's offered to you.

I've turned down way more "opportunities" than I've accepted.

I learned the hard way and wasted so much time on stuff with partners who didn't hold up their end of the bargain or aren't a good fit.

You are your brand; it is critical you protect it with every inch of your being from day one.

KEEP YOUR EYES FIRMLY PLANTED ON THE ROAD AHEAD.

Failed business ideas should be like failed relationships...we should learn from them, vow never to repeat the same dumbass mistakes and then move the hell on.

Dwelling on the "what could have been" is a waste of time; it's done, he has a new girl now and you're on to better things. ☺

Don't spend a day longer than absolutely necessary pouring over why things failed. Take the wisdom and then let it go.

Cry, punch things (not people), get smashed, bore your friends to death with the details but uncover the wisdom and then move the hell on.

You cannot fly when you're weighed down by past failures...just like in love, there is no room for new business (or new love) if your head is in the past.

Wipe the slate clean and start afresh armed with your new-found wisdom.

DO NOT GET CAUGHT UP IN DRAMA AND DETAIL.

We can work ourselves into quite a state if we let ourselves...trust me, I know!

You know how it goes...you open your browser to click on your website, and YOUR SITE'S DOWN!!

In the early days this was akin to life and death for me.

I can still remember my heart racing as the panic set in, I mean, I WAS RUNNING A 3 DAY SALE FOR GOD'S SAKE!!

I'd be on to my tech team, unraveling more and more as each second ticked by.

To find a broken link filled me with dread as I created a story in my mind about how many clients I'd lost who were never coming back, ditto for typos.

Events I had to cancel because no one bought tickets.

Missing a self-imposed deadline.

It ALL felt like life or death, but in reality it was but a blip.

Ask yourself "will this matter a year from now?"

I promise you 99.9% of the time, the answer is no.

Work hard to stay in vision and avoid the detail and the drama. We can't totally ignore the drama itself if it requires attention, but we can manage the scale of catastrophe we assign to it.

Will it matter a year from now?

Can you do anything about it?

Yes - do that.

No - move on.

REMEMBER TO ENJOY LIFE.

It is soooo important to remember to LIVE your life...to enjoy simple pleasures and indulge in luxury every day, to enjoy what you've created TODAY.

We can get so caught up in building our entrepreneurial empire we forget to actually LIVE the life we're creating.

When you have your head down and your bum up in productivity, bad stuff can happen.

Not life or death stuff, but stuff that sucks the richness out of life.

We often lose our joy and become so serious and bent on success that we forget our love of beautiful things. In the rare moments when we look up and realise we're missing out on the fun stuff of life, we tell ourselves we will make time for that when we have finished "X."

The problem with this is that "X" is never finished or when it is there is "Y" screaming for our attention.

This is a life, but is it living?

Is this life a fully engaged life rich in experiences?

Nope, it's not.

REMEMBER WHY YOU BECAME AN ENTREPRENEUR TO BEGIN WITH.

I'm guessing there were images of you bikini clad hanging out on Necker Island with Richard or (and?) dressed impeccably while attending expensive events reigning supreme.

Also, remember your WHY...remember you wanted to change the world for the better, you wanted to add value to the lives of others, you wanted to make a difference.

Have you forgotten this stuff?

Have you forgotten what you were working towards in the first place?

Did you forget that your business was the means by which you were to achieve a lifestyle of luxury and choice and not the lifestyle itself?

I know I sure did!

And then I remembered I wanted a life!

Don't get me wrong I still got out and did things occasionally, but this was the exception rather than the rule.

MY WAKE-UP CALL.

An interesting experience occurred in my accountant's office that was the catalyst for massive change in the way I thought about things.

I'd been putting off catching up with my accountant because I didn't want to know how much I hadn't earned that year. Plus, it was another reminder that I'd been stuffing around for another 12 months without much to show for it.

When I walked in to her office my accountant had my numbers on display via a massive screen; as I sat down I saw a number with around $128,000.00 on the screen.

I was perplexed thinking surely that's not right, surely I didn't produce that income this year.

I had no freaking idea. I thought I was sitting on around $50,000!!!!

So of course despite being ridiculously excited about the fact I'd cracked the $100,000 mark that year, it begged the question...where the hell did all of that money go?????

Well, let me tell you where that money went...

It went on chasing TNBST (the next big shiny thing)...new logos, new websites...half-assed, and never launched business ideas.

WOW...what a smack in the face that was.

I'd been earning excellent money and had no idea. I felt like I was living on struggle street most of the time.

What a wake up call.

It also hit me that all of the beautiful things I thought I couldn't afford yet were not beyond my reach at all.

I could have been living a life of luxury and ease for at least the previous 12 months!!

The stress I'd suffered over my finances was all from my own making.

Crazy hey!!

A FINAL QUESTION

Quick question...Are you a serial launcher??

Then go now and tally up what this little addiction cost you over the last 12 months; you may need wine. See if this isn't the catalyst for you to drill down and discipline yourself to take your current program to full completion.

Remember to enjoy the now...you've worked hard to create whatever it is you have in your life right now so don't let it go to waste.

What do you love about your life as an entrepreneur right now?

What daily indulgences have you been denying yourself that you could in fact be enjoying right now??

Make a list and vow to indulge in the awesomeness you have created (and continue to create) every day.

A life is not fully lived at your desk. Make sure you take time out to stop and smell the roses and to appreciate everything you are working so hard to achieve.

Visit theartofkickingasselegantly.com to find out more about my KAE Programs. http://theartofkickingasselegantly.com/

The Art Of Kicking LOVE Ass

"Being deeply loved by someone gives you strength, while loving someone deeply gives you courage"

Lao Tzu

You may be questioning how someone with 3 failed marriages feels qualified to dispense wisdom on the subject of LOVE, but let me just say this...you can take great comfort in the fact I am TOTALLY across how NOT to do love and that the wisdom I have accumulated on this subject has been learned one painful lesson at a time.

I can't stress strongly enough the impact of finding deep, consuming, passionate love has made on me as a business woman, and that is precisely why I'm including this chapter.

Sounds a bit out there I know but stay with me. ☺

This is a huge topic (in fact, probably a book in its own right!) with a bazillion moving parts to manage and many side roads to get lost down, but I'm going to do my best to cover what I think are the most important love-related parts.

When we talk about love and relationships, the conversation needs to start at where we learned how to love.

I was born in 1969 so in my formative, developing years I was a child of the '70s.

Mum stayed at home, and dad went to work.

Dad made the rules, and they were, in a word... SHIT.

He was a violent alcoholic who had one set of rules for himself and another for the rest of us.

I won't repeat myself explaining my childhood (if you are interested you can read about it in my first book http://www.bulletproofconfidencekickassbody.com/, but in summary here are the love lessons taught to me by my parents.

LOVE = VIOLENCE

LOVE = MISERY

LOVE = TRAPPED

LOVE = HUMILIATION

LOVE = FEAR

LOVE = CONTROL

LOVE = SELF-LOATHING

LOVE = RAPE

LOVE = LIES

LOVE = HIDING

Love certainly did not mean the same to me back then as it does today.

For many, many years I chased love, and I always found it...momentarily at least...and then it was gone.

I had no freaking clue how to do it!!

I knew how to find love (in fact, it always found me), but I had no idea how to sustain it...to be in a relationship and plan to stay!

I also didn't know that I didn't know how to do it!

I put my lack of being able to stay in love down to poor choice of partner, but what it really came down to was 2 things.

1. I had never learned how to love in a healthy way, the way love is meant to be.

2. I had to do A LOT of work to really, truly feel worthy of deep and soul-filling love.

Don't worry, I always thought I was a pretty good catch, and my self-esteem and confidence were seemingly intact. I wasn't wallowing in "Why doesn't anyone love me?" because men did love me, often way too deeply for my liking.

My issues were so deep seeded in how I had learned to love (or not to love) that I was truly oblivious to them or to understanding that there was a different way to go about things.

I'd been working on being who I truly wanted to be for 2 decades, but shit kept happening on the relationship front, leaving clues that I just wasn't there yet!!

Clues like:

Getting married knowing that if (if I'm 100% honest, WHEN) it didn't work out I could get (another) divorce.

Staying with men who loved me, but I didn't love back the way I should convinced that this wasn't their fault but mine, and I owed it to them to make it work.

Before I continue I want to say that (with the exception of 1), every man I have ever been with has been a wonderful person. I do attract great guys. Guys that any other woman would be very happy to live happily ever after with, so this is not a tale of a string of bad relationships with losers with me as the victim...this is about my role in these relationships and how my journey of 100% love and acceptance of myself led to finding the love of my life.

And how you can too if you're looking. ☺

So how do you find (and keep) deep and soul-filling love with a side of toe-curling passion?

And....how does it make you a better entrepreneur?

Let's roll up our sleeves and find out!

KICKING SELF-LOVE ASS

You're gonna hate me for this but you're going to have to rip off a few bandaids, expose a few wounds, and let things bleed for a while.

There will be tears, you will probably want to throw a tantrum like a two-year-old, but it's ok because waiting for you on the other side of the mess is self-love nirvana and trust me, you *really* want to go there. I did, and I'm waiting excitedly for you on the other side with a knowing smile because I know when you pop through on the other side you will be a woman on a mission, completely unstoppable and happier than you've ever been in your entire life.

Let's get dirty!

It took a lot for me to admit that my childhood had an effect on my adult relationships.

I preferred to put it all down to "all men are idiots" and "one day I'll find my Prince Charming, and life will be perfect."

Peeling back the layers and owning my shit was uncomfortable, sometimes excruciatingly so.

It was difficult to look back at the damage I had caused the men who had loved me so much while I was absent, resentful, moody, unlovable and at times, just plain ugly.

Then there's the questioning...

If I knew then what I know now would those relationship outcomes have been different?

For years I was focused on the wrong thing.

I was focused on finding the right partner instead of BEING the right partner.

Being the right partner means coming into a relationship in the best shape possible, and I don't mean physically (although you should want to do that too).

Your number one goal from this point on is this...to fall deeply and completely in love with yourself including your flaws, not in spite of them, because when you can do this then you can truly accept love and also give it unconditionally.

You will attract a partner that is truly a meeting of equals.

I want you to have the greatest love affair you have ever known...**with yourself.**

Once you achieve this, you stand on this earth as a full and complete human being filled to the brim with your own self-worth knowing you are enough...as you are...right here, right now.

When you stand in this space, your energy is magnetic, you glow, you shine, you exude the sort of energy that people want to be around.

Who do you think you will attract when you're in this space?

The same person you would attract hating on yourself and criticizing every thing you think, say or do?

Hells no!

Let's conduct a little visualisation experiment shall we?

Close your eyes...(well not yet, once you've finished reading ☺) and imagine you are heading to a ridiculously high-end, "re-mortgage the house for a cocktail" kinda place for drinks.

You're looking hot, and I mean HAWT! Nope...you're not worried about your muffin top sticking out or your tuck-shop arms...you're rockin your good self like you just don't care, you're channeling your inner sex bomb and loving yourself sick...got it? Excellent!

Not only do you look HOT, you're also feeling pretty sassy...confident, funny, highly intellectual and every word that falls out of your mouth is gold.

You have ZERO attachment to finding a man but look forward to attracting some of the right kind of attention.

Are you with me?

Now..."hot guy" walks away from his mates and comes over for a chat...but he's a wanker...so you elegantly send him on his way.

Hot guy number two sidles up to you at the bar, makes you laugh, buys you a drink, and you have the type of conversation that makes you smile for days.

The evening is full of great conversation and lots of laughs, and when you head home (alone) you're on cloud 9.

Now imagine you're heading to the same bar because your friends are dragging you there kicking and screaming and because you know you need to get out more since you're looking for luurve.

You dress to cover the bits you hate and obsess over your chances of meeting "Mr. Right."

You don't like yourself very much; in fact, there is more than a touch of self-loathing going on. You almost wish you hadn't dumped your ex because you hate being lonely and feel like a loser.

Ok, we're at the bar.

Hot Wanker Guy slides on over, and your eyes light up.

You acknowledge his wanker tendencies, but he's cute and he's probably the best you're gonna get at this point, and besides you're so bloody lonely!!

You go home with him, he doesn't call, you feel shittier than you did before, and you remain stuck on the hamster wheel.

Different attitude, different outcome.

I have seen this play out so many times it isn't funny!!

In the times I've been single and hung out with other single women, I've watched this horror story unfold time and time again, and the result is always the same.

The average person can smell desperation a mile away...in love and in business, the last thing you want to be is desperate.

The way you eliminate feelings of desperation is to detach from the outcome.

The way to detach from the outcome is to love yourself sick.

To know that whether you have someone special in your life or not, YOU ARE ENOUGH.

Pull out your journal girlfriend; you have work to do.

1. Earlier I shared with you what LOVE ='s for me, and now it's your turn.

   LOVE = ??

   Let your thoughts free-fall.

   Keep typing (or writing) until you run out of words then keep going, when you run out again, keep going...there is always more.

2. What did you learn about yourself through the last exercise? Did it shock you?

3. What impact has this had on how you've been loving till now?

4. Is there anything you need to forgive yourself for?

5. What can you do right now to make peace with your "love past"?

Heavy shit isn't it??!!!

It's ok, the hard part is now done and we're movin on.

Time for a shower!

The best part about getting dirty is how you feel after a shower, wouldn't you agree?

I love the feeling of being cleansed, refreshed and renewed after a shower and I'm sure you do too, so now we are going to take a metaphorical shower and emerge feeling totally **amazeballs**!

The shower is your vision.

Your vision for the woman you know you can be: that confident, sassy, gorgeous woman who elegantly kicks ass in life and in love.

Who is she?

Who is she REALLY?

How does she dress?

How does she think?

How does she eat and exercise to look and feel amazing in her own skin?

Where does she go?

What does she do for fun?

Who does she hang out with?

What is one sentence to describe her in all of her sassy, ass-kicking awesomeness?

What do you need to believe to be that woman?

What do you need to let go of to be that woman?

What needs to change for you to be that woman?

Time to Glam Up & Hit the Town!

Feeling awesome??

Well you should! That right there was some hard-ass work, and hard-ass work deserves reward.

Now its time to glam up and hit the town rocking your new Elegant Ass-Kicking Self and no, I don't mean metaphorically! I mean for REALS!! Can you hear my squeals of delight???

Now if you're reading this at 3:00 a.m., I fully understand it's not practical to take yourself out on a little date right now. BUT hey, you're up anyway so you can do the first part and take photos to record the moment!! Yes, you can!!

As soon as you finish reading this, I want you to head straight to your wardrobe and grab an outfit that makes you feel as sexy as hell..heels are compulsory.

Do your hair, go nuts with the makeup, spray your most expensive perfume and don your hottest lingerie (not in that order obviously).

Now you have to leave the house (unless it's 3:00 a.m., in which case you can just record the moment with a selfie and do it all again tomorrow when you won't be mugged).

Yep, you totally do have to do this!!!

Nope, I'm not kidding.

Serious as a heart attack.

Go now! You know what to do and when you come back, I want you to tell me all about it.

Debrief...

Spill the beans...how did this exercise make you feel?

What did you learn?

What are you going to change as a result?

How will this change your life?

KICKING LOVE-ATTRACTION'S ASS

I don't have any problem attracting men...no problem at all, but attracting the RIGHT man? Well...that's a whole other story!

As I mentioned earlier, I do have a knack for attracting good men, men who are honourable, strong, loving, caring, sharing and all of the rest...just not for me (nor me for them even if they couldn't see that at the time).

I don't attract the horror stories told to me by my friends who were in the dating pond the same time I was.

(As a side note to any men who accidentally stumbled into this book...sending photos of your pee pee...NOT COOL!! We know you're proud of your pee pee, but as a rule, women are attracted by what's attached to your boy bits before they are attracted to the boy bit itself. Just a heads up!)

*Thankfully this never happened to me, but I seriously lost count of the women who were on the receiving end of a pee pee text! On a positive note, these often provided the best belly laughs I'd had in ages. ☺

I found it interesting to observe that I attracted a whole other type of the male species to that of my friends, and for that I'm thankful. I'm not sure how I would have handled some of the situations my friends found themselves in! These women were attracting men whose single focus was sex. Nothing wrong with that if you're on the same page, but a bad deal if what you're after is love.

I only attracted men who were also looking for love and a long-term relationship.

At the other end of the spectrum, I observed women reject man after man because he was missing one or two items on the "must have" list; being perfectly formed humans themselves, of course, they could only accept absolute perfection in return.

My man didn't knock me off my feet the first time we met, and neither did the man I dated before him.

What I learned very early on is that first impressions can't be relied upon when it comes to dating: people are nervous and neither of you know the lay of the land. Sometimes it's glaringly obvious from the get-go that this is a "HELL's NO" type situation, but sometimes things require further investigation to be really sure.

The time leading up to meeting the love of my life left many lessons that I know will help you find love - some relevant, some not so much - but take from it what you need and discard the rest Bruce Lee style.

At the end of 2012, I was in what you would call a fairly average situation...in fact, it was shit, no two ways about it.

I had separated from my ex-husband in August and for reasons too boring to explain in more detail, I was recovering from hip surgery and living / sleeping in my home office on my son's old single bed - yep, I was living the freaking dream.

I was absolutely single and ready to date. I'd been in my marriage six years too long, and it had been one very lonely, soul-destroying time...I was off the leash and ready for some fun.

In my head I had visions of lots of steamy sex and dating lots of different men...I gave myself full permission to do this given I could count on one hand how many times I'd had sex in the previous 3 or 4 years...sex drought city!

My vision didn't happen though, turns out that isn't who I am!

Instead, I lived vicariously through my friends' hot and sweaty sex lives knowing my time would come (no pun intended ☺).

Here's the thing.

My living situation was total crap, but I was so damned happy I can't even tell you.

I was freeeeeeee, and the relief of having done what I needed to do was palpable.

I looked amazing (I totally did). I was glowing, and it didn't seem to matter what I was wearing or if I had makeup on or not or if my hair needed a wash or not...I was a magnet, it was pretty heady stuff...but I remained single and sexless...and I didn't care, I was happy.

One night in late November or early December I was out with the girls and got chatting with a guy, and at the end of the night he asked for my number. He was nice enough, but not really my idea of hot stuff.

I gave him my number and went home with my girlfriend.

Long story short: we went on a date later that week and he blew my mind with amazing conversation, became more attractive by the minute, and I filed away in my memory bank that I shouldn't go by first impressions.

He dropped me off after dinner and we organised to catch up again.

That turned into an awesome 5-month relationship. I had so much fun, we were compatible, sex was back on the menu and life was good.

Turns out he wasn't the one, but I have no regrets. Yes, there were tears, but ultimately I learned more about what I did and didn't want in my next relationship and this experience helped me to recognise the potential for a relationship with my gorgeous man.

In the meantime, I had moved out of my home office / single bed situation and into a home of my own (with my kids) and felt really settled and happy.

I spent some time on my own, worked on my "stuff" some more and all of a sudden decided that I was too damn young (ish) and hot (ish) to sit home alone on a Saturday night.

My friends were in relationships by now, so my dating posse had disbanded and I was at a lose end.

I was content on my own, but I also didn't want to miss out on the juice of life that comes from spending time with the right man.

So I signed up for online dating with eHarmony.

It was a slow process, but I wasn't in a hurry.

I met one lovely guy for coffee and while he was a great guy, I knew I would never be physically attracted to him and so that was that.

Things were going sooo slowly, so I decided to broaden my criteria and conducted a "what if" search and came across my man.

His photo was TERRIBLE, but he had taken the time to fill out his personality profile and seemed very interesting.

The deal breaker for me was the fact he was five years younger and had a daughter much younger than my own kids, not really something I had wanted to consider. But this was taking AGES, and I figured why not just go and see.

I lived 50 minutes out of Melbourne, so I lined up two dates the day I met my man (I'm a good multi-tasker) and I met with him first.

We spent almost four hours together, but seriously I was losing the will to live in the first two!! It was awful!!

He was fully aware I had another date and was cool about it and when we parted ways, I was unsure if we would catch up again.

I should say here that my man and I hadn't been in touch much at all, one quick phone call and a couple of texts to organise logistics and that was it.

My second date and I had been texting flat out for days, and he was hilarious and smart and sharp, all very attractive. He was also an entrepreneur, loved travel and was doing pretty well for himself in life.

He was also a class A wanker!!

I couldn't leave fast enough!!

I drove home with happy thoughts though; it was a fun day, it got me out of the house, and this was my first real attempt at dating since my 20s!!

Over the next few days I thought more about that first date, and I was at the gym with my friend when I blurted to her "I think I like him!!'

The more I thought about my first date, the more he grew on me. We hadn't really been in touch since our date, but I texted him letting him know I'd like to catch up again and that I was free the coming weekend (no "The Rules" for me!).

He got back to me right away, and we were on.

We met for dinner in the city, and it was awesome.

He was much more relaxed, and I no longer had a second date hanging over my head as I did at our previous meeting.

By the end of the night we both knew and when Dave kissed me goodnight he was the perfect gentleman.

The next morning Dave came to my hometown, we spent the day together and the chemistry was out of control, again I sent him on his way, and again he was the ultimate gentleman.

We didn't rush things, but we both knew this was it.

We are (at the time of writing) close to two years in, and never in my life have I felt such deep love, passion, connection and ease with a man.

He didn't tick many things on my list, but he's perfect for me and I for him.

He challenges me in ways that open my mind and balances my crazy nature with his relaxed one.

It has taken me forever to find this, but the wait was worth every agonising second.

How did I attract this?

By loving myself, detaching from the outcome and by not accepting anything less than I knew I deserved, and you can do the same.

I know I'm a good person with a lot to give, and I refused to be with anyone who couldn't really see me (not just the way I look) and be willing to be for me what I knew I would be for them, and you too should expect nothing less.

I know I'm loving, loyal and very respectful of allowing my partner to be who they truly are. I don't try to change them, I don't try to control them...I just love them and honour who they are and expect the same in return.

I had set my expectations high, and they were met.

What are your expectations?

Are they based on your deeper needs and desires or on those of society?

Are there things you need to take off your list?

Spend some time in review…what are you holding out for that may no longer be relevant?

What have you been settling for in the past but no longer will?

Did any of the above resonate with you?

What was it?

How can you use this going forward?

KICKING THE ENTREPRENEURIAL SUCCESS / LOVE CONNECTION ASS

I've had entrepreneurial success in my life, and I've also had love in my life....just not at the same time!

I'd been on this rollercoaster of managing crap relationships while trying to build my empire, and let me tell you, it was freaking exhausting!!

I can multi-task with the best of them but when you're trying to tackle two important elements of your life, both of them emotionally charged, there is little room for growth in either area.

Being an entrepreneur is a tough gig. Sure from the outside looking in it's all champagne and roses, but the reality is it's a gut-busting, often soul-destroying road to success.

If you are in a relationship that's sapping the life out of you, your business won't flourish. If your business is successful and you're in a crappy relationship, I promise you there is a whole other level of success you don't even know about.

Again detachment comes into play.

When I've been miserable and lonely in my relationships my number one focus was my business...how I felt about myself was dependent on my success or failure in business...there was nothing else.

The highs were okay but without anyone to share them with they were often kept close to my chest.... and the lows were devastatingly lonely without anyone to share the burden.

Now things could not be more different.

I love my business as much as I ever have, in fact probably more so, but now it's something I DO, and it's no longer who I AM.

I no longer work 12 - 14 hour days to fill a void.

I have so much else going on in my life outside of work these days, and I want to enjoy it.

This means my workdays are far more streamlined, my love holds out his hand for my phone at the end of the day, and I let him have it because my work is done; I don't need to distract myself with work anymore.

My man loves me and is proud of all I do, but he doesn't get excited about much because to him, this is the way I make my living, not the sole focus of my life.

A little while back I called him to tell him I was a featured athlete for The Commando (A male trainer on the Australian version of The Biggest Loser), and that his team was flying down from Sydney to film me for the entire day.

His response: "That's great sweetie."

Me: "That's so cool isn't it babe, are you excited??"

Him: "Babe, if it makes you happy that's great."

Another time..."Babe! I've just been invited to speak at a massive Martial Arts Conference in Florida, my first OS gig, how cool is that??!!"

Him: "That's great babe, how much are they paying you?"

Just kill me!

I'm bouncing off the walls barely able to contain myself, and he's all, "That's nice dear, what are we going to cook tonight?"

I called another time to tell him I was being inducted into the Australasian Martial Arts Hall of Fame...."That's great sweetie, are you happy?"

He cracks me up, but his sense of perspective is perfect because it helps remind me of what is really important in my life: the things beyond my business.

Building an empire is always going to be close to the top of my list, but it is no longer top of the list. My relationship is, as well as my family and friends, the people I want beside me in order to be the best person I can be while living a life of fun and adventure.

I always thought my life partner should be a male version of myself, but I was so wrong.

Dave grounds me so that I can fly, he doesn't want to know the ins and outs of my business, just that I'm happy and the result is that my business has never been more successful. I've never felt more creative in my life; ideas are flowing like water.

The old saying, "Behind every good man is a good woman" is the same in reverse and probably even more important because like it or not, women take business far more personally than men ever will.

When men have success they don't question it, they just put it down to having earned it.

They don't have the same insecurities in business that women do.

They often don't have to juggle the logistics we do either: kids, meals, household, etc.

Female Entrepreneurs go hard and often it costs us dearly in terms of hits to our self-esteem when things don't go to plan and pure, unadulterated exhaustion trying to keep all of our plates spinning in the air and never asking for help because...you know...we can do it all!

Knowing we have a strong man standing behind us telling us we're okay, drawing our attention away from our failures and reminding us there is more to life than business is a good thing because it provides us with a dose of perspective we often sorely need to help us get back on the horse and fight another day.

It's also great for the detachment thing.

When you love yourself and know your worth, failures are simply information to help us launch off in a wiser way next time.

When you back that up with a loving relationship, the bumps in the road are softer.

Besides all of that, a woman in love is a powerful magnet for her desires. We are powerful anyway, but love dials things up a few notches and we can all do with that!

The Art of STAYING in love.

Again this could be a whole other book!

What I know about this relationship and the ones before it is this.

THEN - I was focused on the bits I loathed and that's what grew.

NOW - I focus on the bits that are awesome and this is what grows.

THEN - I had to be right / to win.

NOW - I'm concerned with reaching a solution we're both happy with, to win and see him unhappy feels like a loss.

THEN - I focused on what I wanted.

NOW - I focus on "us" and what "we" want.

THEN - I cracked it every time they left a mess.

NOW - I only do this occasionally (hey, I'm human!).

I can remember my mum saying, "Chose your battles" and this was something I implemented with my kids early on. I've now applied this to my relationship, and it works a treat there too!

In speaking with other women who are still totally, madly, deeply in love with their partners 5, 10 and even 20 years down the track, I could see the things I had started doing were the very things they saw as the keys to a loving and deeply passionate marriage over the long haul.

Other things that came up were…

Making moments count in a busy day.

We can't all sit staring lovingly into our partner's eyes for hours each day, but we can stop what we're doing to hug and kiss hello or good-bye or to truly listen to what the other is saying.

When Dave gets home from work he hits the shower straight away, and I sit on the bathroom floor while he showers and we chat about the day. It's a small moment in time each day that both of us enjoy - it's a ritual these days.

Seeing your lover, not your lazy husband.

There have been many a spill left uncleaned and chairs not properly pushed back in and dishes left for me to clean up since we first met, and it would be very easy for me to get worked up about those things but I made a conscious choice not to.

Yes it drives me insane and yes sometimes there comes a point where I hit the release valve and vent, but mostly I absorb the annoyance because I know that in the grand scheme of things I'm a lucky woman and he's as close to perfect as I'll ever want (seriously...too perfect would be TOTALLY annoying!).

We all have habits our partners aren't crazy about just as some of their less than awesome habits drive us around the bend. But this is not what we want to focus on because if we do our dream man morphs into "lazy husband" and by default we become "nagging wife." Nobody wants that because it's a passion killer.

I work hard to see my man as the one I met sitting in a café by the beach, the one who adores me and thinks I'm hot, and funny, and more than a little crazy in a good way.

If you want a deeply passionate and connected relationship, being in love isn't enough - you have to work at keeping the passion alive.

You want to see the man you fell in love with, and you want him to see the woman he fell in love with.

Don't morph into something else and don't let him either.

Get out of the house.

Our life is pretty good at home: my kids are older and barely home, and Dave's daughter only stays with us at school holidays so we pretty much have the run of the house.

My office is also at the house.

As are the lawns, the washing and the back deck that needs painting.

I think for most of us we don't realise just how much pressure we put on ourselves to do stuff when we're at home until we go away, and there is nothing to do except hang out with one another.

Even one night away every few months is perfect for taking us out of the everyday and de-stressing with the person we love best in the world.

I swear sometimes we've only been away one night, and I come home feeling as though we've been gone a week (in a good way).

Get away for the night or for a meal or just for a glass of bubbles at the local pub.

Take time away from the stress of your home environment and enjoy one another's company away from the stress, pressure and demands that we face at home, especially if either of you work from home.

If it's been a while since you felt the spark - think back past the annoyances, before the pressures changed your relationship - and remember the passion you felt for one another.

Remember the things you did together that made you laugh.

Remember back to when you couldn't wait for him (or him for you) to walk in the door.

Remember when you would sit for hours and talk and laugh.

Without the current stresses and pressures you're under right now, how would your relationship look?

Also, how would the stresses and pressures in business feel if your relationship was everything you wanted it to be?

In a nutshell.

Every woman deserves to find a deep and passionate love, to experience deep connection with her man.

Every woman should be with a partner who makes her feel amazing, loved, connected.

She deserves to know that her man has her back.

That she is loved unconditionally.

No woman should settle.

No woman should remain in a relationship where she feels diminished.

Love yourself so you can allow love in.

Love yourself so you don't attract rubbish.

Love yourself so when you do meet the right person, it is an equal meeting of minds and wills.

And finally the answer is always love yourself first, so you can allow others to love you fully as well.

The Art Of Kicking MONEY Ass

We do not "make" money. We create and open pathways to the flow of the energy of money"

Dyan Garris

Oh boy, is this a hot topic!

Second to love, MONEY was the other nightmare I couldn't get under control.

As you already know from the previous chapters, I'd had a six-figure business for a while and didn't even know it!

THAT is how clueless I was about my money...the stuff I was hustling so hard for and for so long!!

I was constantly broke; whether I brought in $500 or $15,000 that week, I was always scraping the bottom of the barrel.

When I had money I spent it, and when I didn't, I still managed to spend it.

It got so bad that in 1999, as a single mum caring for two young children, I went bankrupt.

The stress I caused myself around this time was ridiculous, and looking back I now know it was also unnecessary.

The reason for the bankruptcy was in large part because I let my ex-husband walk all over me in our settlement. He then chose not to support our kids financially, so I was on my own and I was struggling.

I'm not playing victim: I was a dumbass about everything finance-related and in the settlement only wanted peace.

I chose peace over fighting for what was rightfully mine.

He now sits happily on the waterfront property we purchased together, with its value around the 2-mill mark. We purchased it for 60 grand.

I'm not bitter at the loss of money or that he took advantage of the fact I was taking care of a baby and a toddler, was totally exhausted and stressed out, and only wanted peace.

Nope…not angry about that, but I am still borderline angry that I hadn't educated myself when it came to money and that I didn't value myself enough to fight for what was mine.

It happened again when I went into business with another man I was in a relationship with. I sought the purchase of the business and had all of the qualifications (it was a gym) and people skills to make it work.

Because of the bankruptcy I wasn't eligible for a loan so my name was nowhere to be seen in the business documents. We broke up, and once again he was sitting pretty and once again I was left starting over...with nothing to show for my efforts.

My last two marriages?

Same deal.

Why did I put myself through this again and again?

Self-worth, or lack of it.

I felt such shame about the bankruptcy, but it went deeper than that.

Just like in love, we learn how to view and manage money based on what we're taught as kids.

We sat on the poor side of the fence, so I was the kid in primary school with the ass out of her pants.

I was the kid with the bad teeth.

I was the kid without the free spirit many of the other kids possessed in my classes because they were free from worry.

Money and cool things were not for me.

I was not worthy or valuable enough.

My mum would be HORRIFIED if she knew this because this is not the lesson she would have liked to impart, but her hands were tied. My dad called the shots, and that meant the dollars went on his stuff.

One of my earliest memories of feeling like a cool kid was in about grade 4.

The Blue Light Disco was on, and I was allowed to go for the first time.

Mum was excited, but I wasn't; I was worried about not having anything decent to wear.

My auntie stepped in, and I can remember my mum and my auntie being so excited about my new bubble gummer jeans and slouchy red suede boots and telling me I looked awesome.

I felt like a million bucks, and the kids at the disco were giving me compliments all over the place, telling me how good I looked.

I rocked into school the next morning in my same new jeans and boots feeling on top of the world.

It is a strong and vivid memory, an awesome one. Unfortunately, it was one of the few positive financial ones, but the feelings of confidence that came with that outfit have never left me.

The bad money lessons continued long after my mum left my dad.

My step-dad was an amazing man and loved me to bits, but he was crap with money too.

In my first year of high school, we lived in tents and showered on the foreshore, things were repossessed at regular intervals, and it was a constant state of feast or famine.

I can remember one day my step-dad came home with hundreds of dollars in cash after being paid for a building job. He threw the money up in the air, and we all rolled in it...we were RICH and planning our bright future!!!

It wasn't long before we were eating sauce on toast for dinner again.

This feast and famine cycle became my standard operating procedure, and I didn't even realise I was doing it all wrong.

This was my normal.

Once I left school at 14 and was earning my own money, you can imagine how things went down.

Pay in hand, straight down the street to buy some new music cassette tapes (yup, I'm THAT old) and then off to the shoe shop (my second weakness), and if I had anything left over, you could find me in the makeup aisle at the local supermarket.

I was incapable of keeping excess money; I'd spend 90% of it on payday and scrape by for the rest of the week.

That trend continued my whole working life.

When I stepped into the world of business at 23, I scared the poos out of myself a few times by not managing my money well.

I quickly discovered I had a high level of stress around owing money and that paying my bills had to be my priority.

I had always paid my bills until things unravelled badly in the lead up to my bankruptcy.

The next phase of my money journey was always having "just enough."

Often just enough turned to not enough because I was clearly uncomfortable with any excess.

Dave often calls me a "tripper," and I can hear his voice in my head right now telling me "you're a tripper, babe."

It does not make any sense at all when you look at this stuff logically, but money (for women) is about energy (and the emotions we attach to it) and for many of us money is bad juju.

I'm so proud of this new breed of female entrepreneurs who own it.

I love seeing woman after woman declaring her first 20k month or finally hitting 6 or 7 figures, it inspired me like nothing else.

I knew I had more insight, sass and skills than half of these women, and I was sick of being a spectator.

But I didn't know HOW to break through.

I knew I had the ideas, the knowledge and the sense of flair to produce some awesome stuff, but there seemed to be a massive gaping hole between where I was and where I wanted to get to.

Just like finding the love of your life comes down to loving yourself sick, making money - serious money - and learning to manage it starts with your money story.

There are women out there doing a much better job of this topic than I ever could, and one of them is Denise Duffield- Thomas.

I read her book Get Rich Lucky Bitch!, and this firmly set me on the path to generating and managing wealth in a way I had never done before.

You can get a free chapter of Denise's Book HERE https://yu103.isrefer.com/go/grlb/mmhext/

Your Money Story

Okay girlfriend, time to get dirty again.

What is the bad money story from your childhood that holds the most charge for you even now?

What is the best money story from your childhood that still makes you smile?

What impact do you think these stories have on your belief systems around money today?

When you think about money when you were a kid, what patterns can you now see clearly?

What impact do these patterns have on your money story today?

Becoming a money grown-up

In 2013, I had started to make some serious money. In early 2014, this trend continued, and the potential for some shit scary money was high.

So what did I do?

I started to sabotage the shit out of my income sources is what I did.

Some months I was bringing in $30,000, and was there any left at the end of the month?

Hell no!

What did I do with it?

Can't even tell you, I mean I still don't have enough shoes!!

One day it dawned on me that this was a serious problem.

That I could be having the same problems at $30,000 that I was having at $3,000 per month told a horror story.

I called my accountant's phone number at 7:45 a.m. and told her I needed to come in and work my shit out, or I'd waste all of this money I was making. I'd get to the end of the year having had hundreds of thousands of dollars slip through my fingers...again.

I declared, "I need to grow up financially."

This is what led to that meeting where I stared at the screen in amazement at the money I'd earned the year before and had no clue about why my income began to grow at a great rate of knots.

Money Is Energy

When it comes to men and money, money is money; there is no bad money juju, no doubting there is more where that came from or agonising over spending $350 on a pair of shoes.

Men are pragmatic when it comes to money, and women are emotional when it comes to money.

We attach all sorts of things to money, many of them disempowering and almost all of them hold us back.

The greatest revelation I had around money was that I wasn't alone, that in entrepreneurial circles this was in fact the norm, and I wasn't the exception.

I got to see that appearances and reality are worlds apart and that the vast majority were "faking it while making it."

I got to see that money issues knew no prejudice when it came to age, education or upbringing...it got everyone...well, almost everyone.

I was, in fact, part of a much larger financially illiterate sorority that I had no idea existed.

When I could finally put the shame to bed and realise that for the entrepreneurial woman, financial struggle and basic financial dumbass-ness are almost a right of passage, then I could stop feeling sorry for myself and get on with it.

I could stop telling myself the story of:

I don't deserve this.

This is for other people but not me.

I'm not good enough / smart enough / popular enough to be rich.

I'm not worthy.

I don't know how.

etc.etc.etc.bla.bla.bla

I began to tell myself every single day, "You are capable of generating large sums of money in your business" and "Your earning capacity is off the charts."

I had helped many women achieve financial success through business. I knew what it took, until then I just didn't think it applied to me.

I'm a big believer in momentum.

Momentum is where we begin to take massive action, which leads to gaining traction, which then leads to feelings of success...this is where our energy peaks...this is where we just "know" this is it and that awesome things are happening.

You can feel the shift.

I had been in that place more times than I can count.

It was at this point that I found myself distracted by the next bright, shiny thing, the thing that derailed me.

Why??

Do yourself a favour, if you read nothing else outside of this book for the next year, make sure you read Gay Hendricks' The Big Leap, he explains in beautifully.

This book changed my world!

The Big Leap introduces the concept of Upper Limiting.

If you've ever listened to Anthony Robbins, he likens this to our internal thermostat.

The concept suggests that we become accustomed to a certain level of comfort, or in many cases, comfortable with a certain level of discomfort.

When things seem too good to be true, we wait for the axe to fall.

Am I right?

Thoughts of "This won't last" or "That was a fluke" abound, and we convince ourselves that our success is momentary and that we should prepare ourselves for the fall.

Often we create the fall because the waiting kills us!

Gay Hendricks hits the nail on the head when he points out that often: if our business success is off the charts, we'll find a way to mess up our relationship; or that if you find love, the wheels fall off your business; or if both are rocking, then we get sick.

We are uncomfortable with the concept we can have it all, all at the same time, or that we deserve to have it all at the same time.

Think about it...how many times in your life have you been riding a massive wave of momentum only to be dumped unceremoniously on the shore wondering how the hell you got there?

When you're experiencing success it's important to catch yourself upper limiting and nip it in the bud.

These days I recognise my upper limiting for what it is, and in my mind I say, "I know what you're doing, and you can just eff off thank you very much. I made this happen, I deserve my success, and there is plenty more where this came from."

There is a saying...new level, new devil...and it's true.

The same shit surfaces at $30,000 as does at $3,000, and I've heard it's the same at $300,000 and 3 mill!

No one is immune to Upper Limiting so know about it, look for it to rear its butt-ugly head and tell it to piss off. You deserve more, and you can have more.

Momentum is best explained in this sense, as more attracts more.

The enemy to continued momentum is upper limiting.

Kill that sucker dead, and you are well on your way.

We want to feed momentum and kill off upper limiting simultaneously, and over time, upper limiting decreases and momentum increases.

Remember, money is energy, so we need to generate the kind of energy that attracts money...and lots of it!

Your job is to become a money magnet through your business, and we do that by generating the type of energy that feeds the empire-building beast. The type of energy that allows us to tap into the resources we have within ourselves and attract the resources we don't.

We want to get into and remain in a constant state of flow.

This is a place where everything feels effortless and "meant to be"...it is as though everything in the universe is lining up to deliver everything we know we can have.

To generate this kind of energy, we need to feel abundant.

You get what you focus on, so if you are focused on bills coming in, you will get more bills.

In a nutshell, when you focus on the things you don't want, you get more of them.

Thankfully the opposite is also true: when we remain focused on what we DO want, we get more of that. We get more of that until we begin upper limiting, but we know what to do with that pesky little sucker now, so we deal with it in a detached manner and move on.

If you're scraping the bottom of the barrel on a daily basis it's hard to feel rich or abundant or wealthy, or whatever term it is you like to use, but you absolutely MUST generate feelings (energy) of abundance to attract more.

When you feel poor you attract poor.

When you feel rich you attract rich.

I'm not just talking about money here either. When you feel poor (negative), you generate poor thinking and poor habits and attract poor people.

When you feel rich (positive), you generate rich thinking and rich habits and attract rich people.

The people and things you attract into your world are a direct reflection of your own thoughts, so if you have poor thinking there is no way in hell you will attract rich.

Rich people, in all senses of the word, are not attracted to poor people (in all senses of the word).

Successful, happy, energetic, adventurous, wealthy, positive people avoid bad energy like the plague.

We know bad energy attracts more bad energy and ain't no one got time fo dat!

We only want to attract positive people, the ones who bind to us for the purpose of generating even bigger, better energy and momentum.

I've thought about this a lot, and I really had to come to grips with this concept because I'm a kind person and I can sense a wounded bird a mile off.

At networking events I used to feel compelled to "save" these people. I was a magnet to the downtrodden and felt excellent in my role as mentor and savior.

I don't do this anymore, not because I don't care (I do), but I finally recognised this for what it was.

This was me being comfortable with playing small.

I was comfortable being surrounded by people who were like me, or a rung below me on the success ladder.

And it kept me stuck.

The moment I started investing in high-end programs, going to high-end events and mixing with high-end people, my thinking was elevated and so was my income.

Not only were my thinking and income elevated, so were my expectations.

I wanted more, and I was surrounded by women who had more and were in the process of generating even more than that!

Misery loves company and so does success.

Want more money and success?

Then hang out with rich, successful people.

These days I am far from rude at networking events, but I quickly disengage from women who are where I was three years ago and instead seek the ones with my level of success or with greater success.

This is where I need to hang out to ensure my continued growth and success.

The place for the women who need my help is in my programs.

So...where do you start?

After you've come to grips with your money story and all of its wonderful lessons, generate feelings of success and abundance that will get you into a state of flow.

Remember we are seeking to feel abundant, even if our bank balance is in the red.

We also need to clear the space for money and success, and we do this by ridding ourselves of anything that no longer serves us or anything that makes us feel cheap or poor.

When money was tight in the early days, I was still able to generate feelings of wealth, success and abundance, and it didn't cost me a cent.

Things that made me feel abundant and in control were:

A sparkling clean home that was organised and clutter-free.

Fresh flowers, though I couldn't always afford to purchase beautiful fresh flowers like I do now, I would go for a walk around the garden and look for blooms of any sort (even if they weren't my fav) and put them in vases around my home.

If I did have spare cash, I would always purchase a couple of bunches of flowers.

Flowers = Elegance, Abundance and Beauty in my eyes, and this is still a priority today.

Gratitude lists always help me feel rich in every way too. I would look around me and realise I had a whole lot more to be thankful for than many other people in the world.

This dose of perspective always inspires me.

I don't just stop at the "stuff" I own or the wonderful people in my world but also being so grateful for my resilience, for a mind that can generate creative ideas and thinks outside the square, for my capacity to inspire others...I can write a gratitude list for hours if you let me.

Three seemingly small things, but this has always had a profound effect on my energy, allowing me to get into a state of flow that opens the door to an avalanche of opportunities and abundance.

Clearing the space for money and success is important; remember money is energy.

If your thoughts are full of noise and your surroundings are cluttered, rather than be a magnet for money and success, you will be a repellent!

We don't want that!!

So spend some time clearing your acquired clutter, throw out anything that no longer fits, is in a state of disrepair or makes you feel cheap or poor.

Clear the space for all of the good things you want to invite into your world.

The same goes for your thoughts: get rid of thoughts that no longer serve you.

Keep an eye out for the loop of negative thoughts that continually play in your mind.

Can you change it?

If you can, then jump to it.

If you can't, then find a way to let it go and move on.

Keep clearing until you feel a sense of peace.

The Big, Grown-Up Step

The BGUS is getting your financial shizzle in order.

It's making the call to your accountant (or hiring an accountant).

It's about getting real with your finances and finding out exactly where you stand.

It's about having financial clarity.

It's about planning for your financial future.

I promise you that even if the numbers aren't good, once it's all there out in the open, you will feel a wonderful sense of control and optimism.

Becoming a money grown-up is highly liberating stuff, and once you take control over this area of your life, there is no holding your business back so please don't back away from the work required from this chapter.

You can thank me later ☺

The Art Of Kicking
FITNESS Ass

"Take care of your body. It's the only place you have to live"

Jim Rohn

Let me share something with you... I struggled with use of the word "fitness" for this chapter because it suggests the focus is on training. However, what I really mean is how you look and feel as a result of the way you move your body and the foods you put in it...a bit long for a chapter title. ☺

It is also about how we transition from training to working in an elegant manner, so we don't sit about in our sweats all day...this is probably much more of a conundrum for those of us with businesses in the fitness or martial arts industries.

Training and Elegance are at odds with one another and trying to marry the two has caused me much angst over the years.

Kicking the bejeezers out of a bag, running stairs till I vomit and training my little ass off at a fight camp in

Thailand are not très chic by any stretch of the imagination, and there is no way I know of to make it so.

So how do we combine sweat with chic?

The short answer is we don't.

The longer answer is we embrace the contrast and work out a way to move effortlessly between training the house down and sweating like a little piggy and spending the rest of the day looking effortlessly chic as we go about the business of building our empires.

In my day-to-day life it was practical and convenient for me to live in workout gear.

My weekdays consist of training in the morning and again in the evening and in between I was mostly at my desk at home, so I figured it didn't matter if I wore my workout gear day in and day out.

I was comfortable, it was a hassle to change and the hair thing was just all too difficult!

The result of living in sweats wasn't good...nothing life or death, but I noticed I would avoid heading into Melbourne for events because I couldn't be bothered wearing heels!

I found it highly inconvenient to go to any daytime event because it required me to change outfits!

If I really had to attend an event, I'd schedule a rest day so I didn't have to get changed!!!

Seriously??!!

I'd head into Chadstone Shopping Centre (THE Shopping Capital ☺) in workout gear because you know, I was walking and carrying stuff, and this was the most practical thing to do.

I avoided certain shops, telling myself I'd go in next time when I was "dressed up," only I never was.

I put off going out because I hated making the effort.

I spent the weekends in my workout gear - I mean I was going to the gym at some stage that day so why the heck not?!

Without realising it, I had subconsciously determined that fashion and looking good were no longer important to me.

But it was...and it still is.

I know for a lot of women not wanting to dress up and go out is attached to confidence, often centered on body issues, but I couldn't even chalk it up to that.

I scrub up okay, I like my body and look good in great clothes....I just couldn't be bothered and that's just not cool!

I slowly became aware that I was missing out on life because I couldn't be bothered to make the effort, and as one of my higher values is adventure this was a major problem...something had to change.

At the same time I was fighting a constant internal battle that probably seems insanely stupid to most people, but it was a conundrum for me.

Who was I?

How did I see myself?

I holidayed and trained in Thailand and loved it...a lot...I spend my days sweaty, make-up free and fuzzy haired...a big hot mess in the looks dept., but I'm so bloody happy there it's ridiculous. I feel totally at home in Thailand; I'm definitely a more relaxed and serene version of my everyday self, and I enjoy that.

I also adore Paris and after my first visit felt this was my soul home - this was my true essence...well, I had thought that until I went to Thailand...and thought the same thing...but I didn't want to let go of Paris, my affinity with her and the elegance, beauty and luxury associated with her, and I became torn.

So who the hell was I: a Thailand girl or Paris girl??

Surely I can't be both??

Turns out I can and while you may not experience the same ridiculous conundrum (ridiculous because no one set any rules around this; I totally made it up out of nothing) I did, I'm sure you have your own internal battles when it comes to healthy eating and training, even if it is just the struggle of whether or not to get out of your workout gear or not!

When should you train?

How should you train?

Where should you train?

How much should you train?

Then, of course, there's the food...

What should you eat?

What should you cut?

When should you eat?

What supplements should you take?

When should you take them?

If you're a fitness or martial arts professional, you've probably got this sorted and are more concerned with how to integrate a little elegance into your lifestyle. But if you're an entrepreneur trying to build an empire looking for a way to look and feel good about yourself, no doubt you've debated the questions above time and time again...often debated it for so long that you've become overwhelmed and given up!

In the end, you're ALWAYS second-guessing yourself because it is all so damned confusing, and every "expert" has a bigger, better method that they're begging you to try next.

Here is the thing: I've tried many different types of training over the years. I've tried many nutritional concepts over the years and you know what? The difference has always been negligible.

The ONLY thing that has ever made a difference for me was consistency, and consistency has always been maintained more easily through training and eating in a way I enjoyed.

There it is....the magic pill you may or may not have been searching for; find a healthy way of eating and training that you enjoy and stick at it long enough to see a result.

My Little Nutritional Experiment...

For YEARS I had followed the whole eat six meals a day, eat lean protein with every meal, don't go longer than three hours without food approach.

From time to time I'd keep a food log to check I was eating enough and that my macros were about right.

It works, I feel great on it, no problemo....except for the fact that from time to time I lose interest in food because it becomes a case of Groundhog Day.

It was during one of these "episodes" that I thought I'd try something different.

I decided that I would not pre-prepare my meals for the week and instead take the time to prepare yummy fresh meals AND the time to enjoy them.

In France, fresh, seasonal produce is king; the French eat bread at every meal and enjoy wine with most (don't worry, I'm not suggesting this).

I decided to take a leaf out of their book and see what happened.

I remembered my trip to France and Italy a few years before when I ate beautiful Parisian pastries every morning, incredible pizza and wine most nights, and indulged in mouth-watering macaroons on a daily basis.

I had expected to come home with 3 kg of excess baggage in all the wrong areas, but I didn't.

I mostly ate two meals each day, three at the most, and I walked everywhere. The result was nothing changed.

With this in mind, I decided to shake things up.

Oats made with water, coconut oil and protein powder gave way to rye sourdough bread sprayed with olive oil, toasted then topped with red, juicy vine ripened tomatoes, fresh torn basil, Himalayan rock salt, cracked black pepper and buffalo mozzarella melted under the grill.

I left my desk, sat at my beautiful dining table and dined on this beautiful meal that satisfied my eyes, my mouth and my belly.

My midmorning snack of a cold kangaroo burger and sliced capsicum wasn't required because I was still comfortably satisfied from breakfast.

My lunch of reheated chicken breast, brown rice, broccoli and olive oil became Tuna Niçoise Salad or Thai Chicken Larb.

My dinners of lean protein and steamed veggies became more exotic and enjoyable, all made with fresh seasonal ingredients and a lot of love.

I paid no attention to my macros (proteins, fats, carbs, sugars, etc.) or how many hours it was since I last ate and instead focused on creating beautiful meals with good-quality produce, and I have to tell you...life was a whole lot more enjoyable!

It was a little eat, pray, love action but without the weight gain!

The difference?

I stayed lean, maintained my muscle mass (my main concern as I wouldn't be so protein-focused), my recovery was just as good, my energy levels better and my enjoyment factor off the charts.

My cravings reduced, and I felt as though I was back in the land of the living.

It had not occurred to me I was depriving myself in my previous way of fueling my body because I had eaten this way for as long as I could remember and it worked for me. While I wasn't depriving myself nutrient-wise, I was depriving myself enjoyment-wise...experience-wise...my eyes were well and truly opened.

Food was fuel, and I happily ticked along eating foods that fueled my body with little thought to whether I enjoyed it or not.

I enjoyed treat meals and wine but was always mentally tallying the calories and planning how to rid them from my body; this didn't feel like a negative thing, just a lifelong habit I no longer gave much thought.

When I met my gorgeous man things changed...they changed because Dave LOVES to cook, he loves good food and wine, and the pendulum started to swing the other way!

I was still eating "my way" and enjoying "Dave's way" on the weekends, but I was beginning to feel robbed when the weekends ended and I was back on my "food as fuel" wagon.

For the first time in my life I was starting to feel deprived, and I didn't like it.

I began to question why I continued to deprive myself.

I was no longer competing in taekwondo where I was required to fit within a weight division, and I had no plans of strutting my stuff on stage in a spangled bikini so WHY was I continuing to enforce such stringent eating guidelines?

I decided there was a way I could continue to fuel my body AND enjoy the finer things in life when it came to food, and my little experiment proved me correct.

It doesn't matter what nutritional approach you take, there is always the capacity to overindulge. The same thing happened when I ate like an athlete 90% of the time. However, with this approach I am mostly craving-free, and there is no wagon to fall off.

This is a much more enjoyable existence.

What I want you to take away is this....

If what you have been doing isn't working, it's time for a new approach, and this is how we do it:

Throw out every single diet book you own.

Forget every single thing you have learned about nutrition - even the good stuff.

Begin to eat intuitively.

Eat when you're hungry.

Keep a watch on your portion sizes; if you feel full after a meal then next time eat less, if you feel hungry within an hour, eat more...it is no more complicated than that.

Prepare your meals with fresh seasonal produce and lean proteins.

Enjoy treats without guilt; you're not doing anything wrong when you enjoy a salted caramel macaroon (to die for!!). This is called *being normal*.

Notice how balanced you feel.

Pay attention to the waistband on your jeans...are they becoming loose? Then you're on the right track. Or are they becoming tight? Then it's time to change tack - reduce portions, reduce treats, or maybe you need to move more.

Take the time to enjoy your meals, savour every single bite, taste the juicy, red sweetness of vine ripened tomatoes, roll your eyes to the heavens when you indulge in a couple of squares of the best chocolate money can buy.

It's time to enjoy food again.

It's time to stop seeing food as the enemy.

So...no meal plans, no calorie guide, no structure...are you scared??

If you are, that is TOTALLY normal, and I want you to feel the fear and do it anyway...the worst that can happen is you gain a couple of kilograms you get rid of...a better question is what is the BEST that can happen??

Try it and see.

Note: If you are training for competition, either in martial arts or bodybuilding or any other sport, you might want to hold off on introducing these changes until after your comp. I know for me, if I was getting ready for a comp, the stress of introducing the unknown would outweigh any benefits, so leave it for the off-season if you want to give it a try.

So, in a nutshell, try this:

1. Take the time to prepare healthy, flavourful, fresh meals (when you have the opportunity to) and the time to sit and enjoy them fully.

   There are still many, many mornings I quickly prepare my oats, coconut oil, protein powder and banana breaky to have at my desk when I'm time poor. This is now a conscious choice based on the day, and no longer my default. While it would be nice to sit out on my back deck listening to the birds sing over a carefully prepared breakfast every day of the week, it ain't gonna happen. We need to ensure this works for us given the day we have ahead of us; it's all about finding the balance and not being a slave to any one method.

2. Notice what impact this has on your enjoyment factor AND your cravings.

3. Monitor how your body feels, how you perform, what impact it has on your weight and make adjustments accordingly.

I'm human and sometimes larger portions creep in or I indulge in too many treat foods, and I can feel a muffin top forming. When this happens I switch back to my old way of eating for a few weeks to reset before once again restoring the balance (the new balance).

Training...

I'm a fan of training till I vomit, but I know this isn't for everyone. ☺

The first thing I want to say about training is this...a walk is lovely, and you should definitely walk to relax, fire up the brain cells and be one with nature, BUT walking isn't "training."

If you aren't the sort of person who likes to push yourself in training then I know it will take some convincing, but there is no better feeling in the world than finishing a training session that almost kills you.

It's empowering, it's energising, and when you're done you feel a million bucks.

I'm going to encourage you to indulge in the type of workout that makes you want to cry for mummy at least twice a week. Five training days a week is the required minimum, but you don't need to bury yourself every single session.

I've been training and instructing Marital Arts and fitness for close to 24 years, and I can count on one hand the women I couldn't convert to this way of training.

When a client finishes a workout they never dreamed being capable of in a million years, something shifts.

They develop what I call "The Eye of the Tiger."

We've all witnessed either friends or colleagues who were once ambivalent about exercise and healthy eating suddenly transform before our very eyes.

They've developed The Eye of the Tiger.

They've found their training sweet spot.

The sweet spot is where they've discovered their WHY, the reason they are now ready to make sacrifices, and they've also discovered a way to achieve their dream body that is doable and enjoyable.

When this happens, there is usually no stopping them.

When you taste that high of smashing a workout and the empowerment that comes from it, there is no going back.

If this isn't your usual way of training then this can seem downright scary, but I'm here to tell you the thought of it is worse than the reality.

You don't need to launch into a vomit-inducing session right off the bat.

Start by adding bursts of intensity to give yourself a taste and then work your way up.

If you're a walker try adding 5 x 30 second runs into your walk, then make it 10, then make them 20 sec sprints, then 30 sec sprints, then walk to warm-up and make the whole of your session sprints then walk to cool down.

It would be unreasonable (and unenjoyable) to expect you to go from walking 30 minutes a day to 30 min of sprints....you'll die and never want to do it again, and that's not what we want.

Find the point where you can enjoy pushing yourself a little harder and be conscious of the need to raise the bar on this at regular intervals.

Give yourself something to aim for, so you know you're actually moving forward week to week.

Before you know it, you will enjoy pushing your body to new limits and how this makes you feel.

Your new measure will be how your body performs, and you will become interested in beating your times, lifting heavier and recovering faster.

Your measure will no longer be the scale...and this is always the ultimate goal in my book.

A word on consistency...

When it comes to training and nutrition, consistency is the determining factor for success.

Remember this...the food and training you are giving your body will show up a month from now...not in a week.

Essentially you are a month behind the 8 ball from the get-go.

I know you want instant results, to lose 3 kg a week Biggest Loser style, and some of you may experience good results quickly. But this is not the norm, especially if you're in your 30s and beyond.

Typically you won't see any visible results for anywhere between 4 and 12 weeks. (I know, sucks right!?)

Does this mean you quit?

Hells no!

Continue to remind yourself that you are focusing on progress, NOT perfection, and that with consistent effort you WILL see results. You just need to be patient and hang in there long enough to see the rewards for your effort.

Every time you quit, you slow or even halt the process and delay the very results you're working so hard to achieve.

Every time you decide to work out when you can't be bothered and every donut you say no to has a positive impact over time.

Day in and day out, be consistent.

Train hard.

Nourish your body with fresh, healthy meals.

Nourish your mind with positive afformations (you didn't read that wrong, google afformations).

Journal every morning and remind yourself of how important your goals are and again at night as you pat yourself on the back for a day well lived.

Celebrate your progress and feel good about the path you're on.

A word on the perfect training plan....

Umm...there is no one perfect training plan...there just isn't.

Women's bodies are sooooo different.

I'm thin and must weight train regularly to maintain an athletic physique.

Other women just need to look at a dumbbell and their delts pop.

Your body will dictate the best plan to follow. But honestly, unless you are the type of woman who grows muscle just looking at a weight bench or is super thin regardless of how much you eat, then any plan with a good balance of resistance, cardio and flexibility will suffice....IF you follow it.

I have programs at http://RipItUpChallenge.com that get you training my way of training. They are very reasonably priced, and each program has a number of levels so you can start the program regardless of your fitness level.

There are also plenty of free programs online now.

Simply pick one and stay the course.

In a nutshell:

You must train hard and push yourself fully on at least two training sessions per week.

Walking is NOT training.

Consistency is key - whatever program you chose to follow...follow it all the way through.

This doesn't mean do it perfectly 100% of the time, but it does mean don't chop and change between programs on a whim.

Having a program to follow does three highly beneficial things:

1. It gives you structure, as just rocking up to the gym on any given day without a plan is wasting your time.

2. If it is a good program, it will have recovery phases built in so you don't over-train and become injured.

3. It allows you to easily track your progress (Rip It Up Challenge Programs have a fitness test each month so you can easily see your improvement) and set goals to keep you inspired.

The nutshell in the nutshell:

We tend to overcomplicate things, and this leads to questioning everything we put in our mouths and/or every training session we do and this leads to switching and changing erratically.

At the heart of it: train hard, eat well and be consistent...it really isn't any more difficult than this for the average person. Athletes require a more scientific approach, but for the average person, this is where it's at.

Go forth on your adventure of uncovering what works best for you and your body and have fun with it.

The Art Of Kicking
A LIFE WELL LIVED Ass

"Create a life you can't wait to live"

Zig Ziglar

This chapter has been my procrastination chapter because...well...seriously, how HUGE is this topic??!

In fact, after typing the line above, I felt the strong desire to call my mum for a chat. It was a nice little distraction for 10 minutes, but now here we go!

So what IS a life well lived?

Every woman's definition is going to be different because we all value different things with varying degrees of intensity.

So I'm going to tackle this chapter in the only way I know how and that is by using my own definition as a jumping off point and seeing where that takes us. ☺

I believe that while, as women, each of us are unique and have our own quirks, we share many universal desires.

- Travel.
- Luxury.
- Glamour.

- Fun.

- Adventure.

- Love.

- Connecting with people who share our passions.

- Looking good.

- Feeling good.

- Excitement.

- Certainty.

In my experience, we are as alike as we are different.

I once met an aid worker who shared with me that wherever she had travelled to in the world, even in the most desperate of places, the women still spoke of love, romance, and fashion—all things girlie....it seems this is part of our very (fabulous) fabric.

My idea of a life well lived is about no regrets.

I don't know about you, but I want to leave no stone unturned in this life.

Fulfilling my greatest potential in all areas and squeezing as much juice out of life as I can is where it's at for me.

I don't want to die wondering.

I never again want to hear myself say, "I wish I had."

I wish I had worn that damned dress before it went out of style.

I wish I had spent more time looking into my daughter's face and listening to every word she had to say.

I wish I'd been less of a stress head.

I wish I'd allowed myself to have more fun.

If you're not careful, you can wish your life away.

At 45 I can look back over the wonderful canvas that has been my life...I know for sure that it has been well lived.

I've traveled HEAPS, alone, with groups, with my love, with my bestie, with my kids...and I plan to keep on doing this forever and ever and ever (and ever)!

I have so many happy memories and adventures from my travels, and I'm always planning my next trip to somewhere. In six weeks I'm heading back (solo) to my favourite part of Thailand where I train at a Muay Thai gym for hours every day, indulge in two-hour massages, eat clean, healthy food, sip on fresh coconuts and recharge my batteries.

Four and a half months after that, I'll be in the USA again and visiting Florida for the first time when I speak at a Martial Arts Conference.

Later in the year, I'll be back to Thailand running a group tour AND spending time in Paris.

When I was 20 I learned to fly a plane. I've flown in private jets, and for a while I was in aerobatic planes as often as I could hitch a ride. I've also flown in helicopters, powered hang gliders and even an old warbird. Once I've flown in a seaplane, I'll have the full set. ☺

I launched a business in the Paladium Room at Crown Casino in Melbourne (where they host the Logies and the Brownlow Medal) and stood centre stage in front of a full room of women at an event I coordinated to perfection despite NEVER having done it before. Oh, and I was wearing that year's Gown Of The Year. Totally, bloody cool!!

I've given keynotes that made a room laugh and cry, and I've attended events where I've witnessed some AMAZING keynotes.

I have fought full contact fights (in competition of course, not just randomly on the street) and have won (and lost).

I've given birth (twice) and despite my deepest fears still remained "me" and not some softer mummy version of me.

I ran the Paris Marathon.

I've dined in some of the best restaurants in the world.

I've drunk a $1,000 bottle of champagne (not the WHOLE bottle, they made me share).

I've trained in fight camps in Thailand.

I've holidayed in the south of France.

I've indulged in the luxury and cosmopolitan fabulousness of Rome.

I came stone, motherless last in my first Olympic triathlon (long story, it's in my first book), and I didn't die.

I've had stimulating conversations with some of the sharpest minds on the planet.

I've experienced deep, soul-connecting love.

I've had my heart broken.

I've broken hearts.

I've laughed till I almost peed my pants.

I laughed so hard I did pee my pants!

I've cried so hard I thought I'd never be able to stop.

I've raised teenagers...the good, the bad, the ugly.

I've launched businesses that brought great success.

I've launched and bombed...more than once.

I've self-published books, the first of which was a painful ripping off of a Band-Aid I'd laid over my wounded childhood.

You could say I've given life a red hot go, and I'm not done yet.

There is still so much to do, but these days I'm no longer in a rush to do it all NOW!!

Slowing down and finding enjoyment in the smallest of things brings me immense pleasure these days...far more than I ever expected to find given my adrenalin-junkie personality.

Making time for simple pleasures has brought with it a whole new level of richness to my life.

It makes the time in between life's adventures fulfilling, when once upon a time I was just biding time until the next trip, the next launch or the next event.

My life well lived means that if I want to dress up and put my lippy on and try a fancy new restaurant in the CBD on a Tuesday I'll do it; I'll put the feelers out amongst the women I know and say, "Who's up for it?"

It means taking a day off once in a while to wander around the shops to buy my favourite candles and flowers, while going tech-free for the day. Then I'll head home to make myself a beautiful lunch made with the fresh produce I've just picked up from the market.

It means enjoying a glass (or two) of bubbles in a breathtakingly beautiful glass on a Friday afternoon to toast the week gone by and really, truly, deeply give thanks for everything I have created in my life.

It means having the type of conversations that leave you smiling for days.

It means taking risks and putting myself out there.

It means putting enjoyment and experiences ahead of things.

It means playing the game of life full out...with gusto, with passion and in alignment with my vision and values.

Here are some more ways you can live a life well lived....

WEAR THE DAMNED DRESS

It might seem like a small thing to wear your "best" clothes and make an effort with your appearance "just because," but it's really not.

Whenever you create the intention to look fabulous you do so knowing you will feel fabulous as well.

When we look and feel fabulous, our confidence gets a massive boost, and with a heightened sense of confidence, we are more willing to step outside our comfort zone. As you know by now...outside the comfort zone is where the good stuff happens.

As an entrepreneur, image is everything. Women pay attention to women who look fabulous and exude confidence, and they have a MUCH easier time selling whatever it is they do.

If you're an entrepreneur, video is your new best friend, and if you haven't yet embraced video as a way to communicate to your market, then it's time to get on board that train pronto!

Try feeling confident while shooting weekly videos with bad hair...just doesn't work.

Spend time on your appearance so you'll look fabulous on camera, and watch what happens.

Outside of work, the comfort zone thing still applies. Plus when you're feeling sassy and know you look good, your relationship benefits as well.

Instead of lunch out, it becomes a day out because you don't want to go home and sit on the couch when you look so hot.

This means you explore places you haven't before, you're more relaxed and at ease, and a whole lot more fun to be around than the stressed hot mess you might usually tend to be.

If you've ever seen a Rachel Zoe episode, you will notice that she takes absolute delight in every piece of clothing and jewelry she owns.

She intimately knows each piece, knows where she bought it, who designed it, the philosophy behind the design...it's endless.

Each piece is precious and has an equally precious home.

She's like a little kid playing dress-up, and it's so totally fabulous to watch.

Now I'll never be that girl...my passion for fashion simply doesn't run that deep, but I do take more pride in the things I purchase. I also purchase more thoughtfully and house these purchases in a far more respectable way these days.

Rachel Zoe is (stinking filthy) rich, but she's still a mum of young kids and a crazy-busy business woman...she always makes an effort (even though I'm sure she doesn't always feel like doing so), yet it always appears effortless, and we can too, even on a fraction of the budget.

The more you pay attention to the way you look, the easier it gets. You find your fashion feet, know what style works for you and the days of standing in front of your wardrobe in your undies scratching your head wondering what to wear will be a thing of the past.

EXERCISE

- Every day for one month make a super dooper effort with your appearance on workdays and on the weekend.

- Don't go out spending money hand over fist just yet.

- Use this time to rediscover your wardrobe.

- Throw out what no longer fits, is in disrepair or is just plan hideous.

- Keep what you love, and if you need to tidy up your wardrobe so you can easily see the clothing you love and makes you feel good (in time that should be EVERYTHING in your wardrobe), then do that.

- Enjoy the feeling of looking good.

GROOMING

I know...you're thinking...a life well lived is all about how we look???

No, it's not - but trust me - it IS supremely important because this stuff feeds directly into our confidence AND our readiness to accept opportunities that come our way.

What do I mean?

If you're only ever a one-hour spray tan away from being camera-ready, you're going to jump on any opportunity that comes your way...in a heartbeat.

If the thought of being interviewed seems like a hassle because you're 5 kg overweight, your roots need doing and your nails are a mess, you can be sure as hell you're sending "don't come near me" vibes out into the universe, and there is no way in hell opportunity is going to come knocking anytime soon.

I'm far from high maintenance when it comes to my personality, but as for how to keep this rig of mine looking camera-ready, I'm super high maintenance and not ashamed to own it.

Foils, manicures, pedicures, laser hair removal, spray tans, facials and massages all play a part in my week (not everything every week obviously), and I feel a million bucks for it.

Sure, there are those dark days in-between spray tans (when my tan has to come off, so I can get a new one), but the majority of the time I'm ready for opportunity to come a-knocking. In fact, I expect it!

EXERCISE

- Get your grooming house in order.

- Let me ask you...can you throw on your teensy-tiny bikini and head to the pool right now, or does the area down there need some maintenance?

- If you got a phone call from Oprah's team about being interviewed TODAY, could you say "Hell yeah" without reservation, or would you want to turn it down because you aren't "ready"?

- Remember, luck is what happens when preparation meets opportunity.

- Get on top of your grooming stuff and then plug your maintenance visits into your diary and stick to them.

- Investment in your appearance is NEVER wasted, even more so for entrepreneurs.

TRAVEL

I've touched on this already, so I won't need to go into this too much other than to say it's really important to make travel a priority in your life if you truly want a life well lived.

Travel makes life far more interesting, and it also makes you a far more interesting person.

Seeing the world from a different perspective, seeing the way other cultures live and the things they value, muddling your way through a conversation without a common language, finding your way around unfamiliar geography...it's tremendous.

It's interesting.

When you travel, you find your ability to be curious returns.

Your sense of adventure returns.

You feel alive.

Every time I travel I come to appreciate my own country even more.

I appreciate the life I have built here and the opportunities open to us in our very lucky country.

Travel pulls you out of your everyday and creates the space for new thinking.

In business, fresh thinking is priceless.

EXERCISE

- Plan a trip away.

- Where will you go?

- Where will you stay?

- What things will you do when you're there?

- How much will it cost?

- Can you book your accommodations NOW (often when you book online you don't even need a deposit) to show your commitment?

FINE DINE

Recently Dave and I enjoyed a six-course degustation with matching wines.

TO –DIE - FOR!!

Every course was breathtaking.

The waiter / sommelier walked us through every single element on our plates (and in our glasses).

Over four hours, we were taken on a wonderful culinary adventure.

The whole experience was bliss and one we will repeat often, as the restaurant changes the menu every day based on what is growing in the garden and what is fresh at the market in the morning.

We have spent weekends away in absolute indulgence where we've felt cocooned in our own little bubble of preciousness.

Dining in elegance with your girlfriends is also a right of passage as an adult woman.

The conversations that flow are soul fulfilling and nourishing on many levels and gives everyone a boost so they can go back to their lives feeling re-invigorated and reminded of the things that are important to them.

We all have a deep need for connection, and why not do it in style? ☺

LAUNCH

Business will always feature prominently in a life well lived for any entrepreneurial female.

Don't die wondering.

That idea you have that keeps tapping you on the shoulder asking "Is it time yet?" needs to be told, "HELL YES it IS time."

Now don't go running off half cocked...follow the steps I outlined in The Art of Kicking ENTREPRENEURIAL Ass chapter, so you know you have a solid strategy going forwards to give you a better chance of success.

Don't waste weeks or months or years procrastinating over this...start the ball rolling.

It's time to start planning your launch.

A KICKASS BODY

Life is simply too short to live in a body you hate.

We are never going to be 100% happy with the way we look; it's just the way we're made. BUT with a kickass balance of acceptance and work, we can be walking this earth sporting a body we're proud of.

You will be 100 times more excited about embracing "Wear the damned dress" and "grooming" and many other things in life when you're proud of the body you live in.

It takes work, and it can be an overwhelming, frustrating and emotional journey to get there, but I promise you it is worth all of the tears and the tiredness.

EXERCISE

- Go there.
- Do the work.
- Get in shape and feel proud of your body.

BEAUTY

Seeking and appreciating beauty adds peace and elegance to our lives.

When I'm in Thailand, seeking beauty is a game I play.

The town I stay in is a place of contrast.

Rundown huts, dirty and deformed dogs lying in the streets, rubbish everywhere, the barely covered drain that runs along one side of the street.

In contrast, there are some stunningly beautiful buildings in-between the huts. Along one street, someone has built a stick fence, and behind it is lush grass and a row of frangipani trees full of fragrant flowers...it is truly beautiful.

Walking along the street, I can look up and see the majestic Big Buddha sitting atop a mountain.

Regardless of whether the home is a hut with a dirt front porch or a stunningly ornate concrete structure, the pride is the same.

The Thai people constantly sweep and pick up leaves and polish things.

They take a lot of pride in the things they own...we can learn a great deal from them.

Traveling from the airport into Paris was an eye opener: gypsy squats lined the highway and on the streets of Paris were many, many beggars...I know women who have been to Paris and this soured the experience for them. They now vow never to go back, which is such a shame because there is no place in the world like Paris...there is much beauty to be had there.

Now when I drive to or from Melbourne Airport to my home, I appreciate the beauty and cleanliness of the thoroughfare we have created for visitors to our country. ☺

Fresh flowers, a favorite candle, a drive along the coast, a carefully put together meal, a breathtaking work of art, a spotless kitchen, the perfect blow wave, the early morning sunrise, dew on a flower on your early morning walk...there is beauty to be found everywhere.

If you can't get out, spend 20 minutes on Pinterest and be carried away by the beauty to be found there.

Beauty isn't necessary for us to survive on the planet, yet it adds richness and elegance along with a sense of wonder and feelings of peace.

EXERCISE

- Cast your memory back to yesterday.

- What beauty did you overlook?

- What were you so busy doing that you forgot to take in the beauty of your surroundings?

- For the next three days, be on alert for beauty.

- When you find it, stop and take time to appreciate the beauty before you.

- How does this make you feel?

- What does it add to your day?

BE OPEN TO ADVENTURE AND OPPORTUNITY - SAY YES

Don't be so quick to say NO.

Don't be so caught up in the day-to-day of life that you miss out on opportunities staring you right in the face.

Begin to say yes to the things you would normally say no to.

Be open to trying things that scare you.

The comfort zone is a scary place: okay to visit, but we don't want to live there because it's a dead end.

Be sure to constantly challenge yourself to keep growing and expanding through the adventures and opportunities that present themselves to you.

As I suggested at the start of this chapter, a life well lived is highly subjective.

Some of the things I deem important won't be to you and that's okay...it is, after all, YOUR life...so you get to determine what a life well lived looks like for you.

And now you get to put pen to paper and design it.

Let me share a secret with you.

The opening scene of my book was once my vision.

When I was post-op sleeping on my son's old single bed in my home office separated from my husband, this life was just a dream.

It only became my new life in the making when I started to take action.

I got 100% clear on what I wanted, and I worked my ass off until it became reality.

I took a lot of hits along the way, and some of them stopped me dead in my tracks for weeks. But I got my ass back up off the turf, dusted myself off, fortified myself with my vision and again started striding purposely in the direction of my dreams.

I'd love to be able to tell you that there's a shortcut to this thing.

That you don't need to set goals AGAIN.

That you don't need to write out your perfect life 12 months from now AGAIN.

That you won't struggle.

That you won't fall down.

That it won't be hard.

That you will nail your launch, and it will be a raging success on the first go.

That you will find love immediately and without having to kiss a few toads along with way.

That building a body you're proud of is easy.

I can't tell you any of that because I'd be lying.

But I can tell you it's supposed to be hard, and it will all be worth it.

It's supposed to almost break us.

It's supposed to challenge us.

Why?

Because it's a test.

How bad do you want this perfect life?

What are you prepared to sacrifice?

What are you willing to give up in order to have your dreams come true?

Have you ever tested a new love?

We all do it - whether we do it consciously or not, we do it.

How far can I push him (or her) before they say enough?

Are we worthy?

Just like the way we pushed our parents when we were kids...how far can I go before mum loses her shit?

Life is playing its own version of this test.

So...how bad do you want it?

Bad enough to take some risks?

Bad enough to do the work?

Bad enough to start to tackle things differently?

Bad enough to endure a "re-do" of some of the stuff you've already done?

If the answer is YES, then go forth and Kick Ass Elegantly on your way to creating the life (and business) you wish for.

If the answer is NO, then I can't help you, my friend. Until you place enough value on living a life you dream of, nothing I can do or say will get you there...so put the book away...try living your life the way it is for a while longer and when you can't endure it any more, read this book again...knowing we will once again land here, and you once again have a decision to make.

Either way, I hope I have challenged your thinking in some way.

I hope I have inspired you to think big and go for it.

I also hope to assist you in building your Kickass life and business through my programs and hope to hear from you on social media.

This book has been an absolute pleasure to write. I sincerely hope you have enjoyed reading it as much as I enjoyed writing it.

For now...go forth and kick some business and life ass (elegantly, of course).

About Michelle

Michelle Hext is an author, international speaker and Business & Brand Strategist from Melbourne Australia.

She is the founder of TheArtOfKickingAssElegantly.com

Michelle runs her signature 12 Month Luxury Business & Lifestyle Mastermind live around Australia and also works with female entrepreneurs globally through online programs where she helps entrepreneurial women Launch, Rebrand & Grow their businesses.

She is driven to ensure entrepreneurial women create brands and offerings that honour the vision they set out to achieve and is passionate about two things in particular...Being Profesh & Doing Things Properly.

Having been an entrepreneur for over 20 years and owning businesses across a number of industries Michelle has made the mistakes for you and learned the smoothest past to success.

If you're looking to Launch or Rebrand a Kickass Business AND have a life filled with love, luxury and adventure be sure to check out her programs at theartofkickingasselegantly.com

Michelle is also the founder of:

- The Honourable Martial Arts Entrepreneur (michellehext.com)

- RipItUpChallenge.com

- PUSHtkd.com